F. Marion Crawford

Ave Roma Immortalis Vol.I

© 2025, F. Marion Crawford (domaine public)
Publisher : BoD · Books on Demand, 31 avenue Saint-Rémy, 57600 Forbach, bod@bod.fr
Print : Libri Plureos GmbH, Friedensallee 273, 22763 Hamburg (Allemagne)
ISBN : 978-2-3224-9774-4
Dépôt légal : Avril 2025

Ave Roma Immortalis Vol.I

By
F. Marion Crawford

Ave Roma Immortalis

I

The story of Rome is the most splendid romance in all history. A few shepherds tend their flocks among volcanic hills, listening by day and night to the awful warnings of the subterranean voice,—born in danger, reared in peril, living their lives under perpetual menace of destruction, from generation to generation. Then, at last, the deep voice swells to thunder, roaring up from the earth's heart, the lightning shoots madly round the mountain top, the ground rocks, and the air is darkened with ashes. The moment has come. One man is a leader, but not all will follow him. He leads his small band swiftly down from the2 heights, and they drive a flock and a little herd before them, while each man carries his few belongings as best he can, and there are few women in the company. The rest would not be saved, and they perish among their huts before another day is over.

Down, always downwards, march the wanderers, rough, rugged, young with the terrible youth of those days, and wise only with the wisdom of nature. Down the steep mountain they go, down over the rich, rolling land, down through the deep forests, unhewn of man, down at last to the river, where seven low hills rise out of the wide plain. One of those hills the leader chooses, rounded and grassy; there they encamp, and they dig a trench and build huts. Pales, protectress of flocks, gives her name to the Palatine Hill. Rumon, the flowing river, names the village Rome, and Rome names the leader Romulus, the Man of the River, the Man of the Village by the River;

and to our own time the twenty-first of April is kept and remembered, and even now honoured, for the very day on which the shepherds began to dig their trench on the Palatine, the date of the Foundation of Rome, from which seven hundred and fifty-four years were reckoned to the birth of Christ.

And the shepherds called their leader King, though his kingship was over but few men. Yet they were such men as begin history, and in the scant company there were all the seeds of empire. First the profound3 faith of natural mankind, unquestioning, immovable, inseparable from every daily thought and action; then fierce strength, and courage, and love of life and of possession; last, obedience to the chosen leader, in clear liberty, when one should fail, to choose another. So the Romans began to win the world, and won it in about six hundred years.

By their camp-fires, by their firesides in their little huts, they told old tales of their race, and round the truth grew up romantic legend, ever dear to the fighting man and to the husbandman alike, with strange tales of their first leader's birth, fit for poets, and woven to stir young hearts to daring, and young hands to smiting. Truth there was under their stories, but how much of it no man can tell: how Amulius of Alba Longa slew his sons, and slew also his daughter, loved of Mars, mother of twin sons left to die in the forest, like Œdipus, father-slayers, as Œdipus was, wolf-suckled, of whom one was born to kill the other and be the first King, and be taken up to Jupiter in storm and lightning at the last. The legend of wise Numa, next, taught by Egeria; her stony image still weeps trickling tears for her royal adept, and his earthen cup, jealously guarded, was worshipped for more than a thousand years; legends of the first Arval brotherhood, dim as the story of Melchisedec, King and priest, but lasting as Rome itself. Tales of King Tullus, when the three Horatii fought for Rome4 against the three Curiatii, who smote for Alba and lost the day— Tullus Hostilius, grandson of that first Hostus who had fought against the Sabines; and always more legend, and more, and more, sometimes misty, sometimes clear and direct in action as a Greek tragedy. They hover upon the threshold of history, with faces of beauty or of terror, sublime, ridiculous, insignificant, some born of desperate, real deeds, many another, perhaps, first told by some black-haired shepherd mother to her wondering boys at evening, when the brazen pot simmered on the smouldering fire, and the father had not yet come home.

But down beneath the legend lies the fact, in hewn stones already far in the third thousand of their years. Digging for truth, searchers have come here and there upon the first walls and gates of the Palatine village, straight, strong and deeply founded. The men who made them meant to hold their own, and their own was whatsoever they were able to take from others by force. They built their walls round a four-sided space, wide enough for them, scarcely big enough a thousand years later for the houses of their children's rulers, the palaces of the Cæsars of which so much still stands today.

Then came the man who built the first bridge across the river, of wooden piles and beams, bolted with bronze, because the Romans had no iron yet, and ever afterwards repaired with wood and bronze, for its sanctity, in perpetual veneration of Ancus Martius, fourth King of Rome. That was the bridge Horatius kept against Porsena of Clusium, while the fathers hewed it down behind him.

WALL OF ROMULUS WALL OF ROMULUS

Tarquin the first came next, a stranger of Greek blood, chosen, perhaps, because the factions in Rome could not agree. Then Servius, great and good, built his tremendous fortification, and the King of Italy today, driving through the streets in his carriage, may look upon the wall of the King who reigned in Rome more than two thousand and four hundred years ago.

Under those six rulers, from Romulus to Servius, from the man of the River Village to the man of walls, Rome had grown from a sheepfold to a town, from a town to a walled city, from a city to a little nation, matched against all mankind, to win or die, inch by inch, sword in hand. She was a kingdom now, and her men were subjects; and still the third law of great races was strong and waking. Romans obeyed their leader so long as he could lead them well—no longer. The twilight of the Kings gathered suddenly, and their names were darkened, and their sun went down in shame and hate. In the confusion, tragic legend rises to tell the story. For the first time in Rome, a woman, famous in all history, turned the scale. The King's son, passionate, terrible, false, steals upon her in the dark. 'I am Sextus Tarquin, and there is a sword in my hand.' Yet she yielded to no fear of steel, but to the horror of unearned shame beyond death. On the6 next day, when she lay before her husband and her father and the strong Brutus, her story told, her deed done, splendidly dead by her own hand, they swore the oath in which the Republic was born. While father, husband and friend were stunned with grief, Brutus held up the dripping knife before their eyes. 'By this most chaste blood, I swear—Gods be my witnesses —that I will hunt down Tarquin the Proud, himself, his infamous wife and every child of his, with fire and sword, and with all my might, and neither he nor any other man shall ever again be King in Rome.' So they all swore, and bore the dead woman out into the market-place, and called on all men to stand by them.

They kept their word, and the tale tells how the Tarquins were driven out to a perpetual exile, and by and by allied themselves with Porsena, and marched on Rome, and were stopped only at the Sublician bridge by brave Horatius.

Chaos next. Then all at once the Republic stands out, born full grown and ready armed, stern, organized and grasping, but having already within itself the quickened opposites that were to fight for power so long and so fiercely,— the rich and the poor, the patrician and the plebeian, the might and the right.

There is a wonder in that quick change from Kingdom to Commonwealth, which nothing can make clear, except, perhaps, modern history. Say that two thousand or more years hereafter men shall read of what7 our grandfathers, our fathers and ourselves have seen done in France within a hundred years, out of two or three old books founded mostly on tradition; they may be confused by the sudden disappearance of kings, by the chaos, the wild wars and the unforeseen birth of a lasting republic, just as we are puzzled when we read of the same sequence in ancient Rome. Men who come after us will have more documents, too. It is not possible that all books and traces of written history should be destroyed throughout the world, as the Gauls burned everything in Rome, except the Capitol itself, held by the handful of men who had taken refuge there.

So the Kingdom fell with a woman's death, and the Commonwealth was made by her avengers. Take the story as you will, for truth or truth's legend, it is for ever humanly true, and such deeds would rouse a nation today as they did then and as they set Rome on fire once more nearly sixty years later.

But all the time Rome was growing as if the very stones had life to put out shoots and blossoms and bear fruit. Round about the city the great Servian wall had wound like a vast finger, in and out, grasping the seven hills, and taking in what would be a fair-sized city even in our day. They were the last defences Rome built for herself, for nearly nine hundred years.

Nothing can give a larger idea of Rome's greatness than that; not all the temples, monuments, palaces, public buildings of later years can tell half the certainty8 of her power expressed by that one fact—Rome needed no walls when once she had won the world.

But it is very hard to guess at what the city was, in those grim times of the early fight for life. We know the walls, and there were nineteen gates in all, and there were paved roads; the wooden bridge, the Capitol with its first temple and first fortress, the first Forum with the Sacred Way, were all there, and the public fountain, called the Tullianum, and a few other sites are certain. The rest must be imagined.

RUINS OF THE SERVIAN WALL RUINS OF THE SERVIAN WALL

Rome was a brown city in those days, when there was no marble and little stucco: a brown city teeming with men and women clothed mostly in grey and brown and black woollen cloaks, like those the hill shepherds wear today, caught up under one arm and thrown far over the shoulder in dark folds. The low houses without any outer windows, entered by one rough door, were built9 close together, and those near the Forum had shops outside them, low-browed places, dark but not deep, where the cloaked keeper sat behind a stone counter among his wares, waiting for custom, watching all that happened in the market-place, gathering in gossip from one buyer to exchange it for more with the next, altogether not unlike the small Eastern merchant of today.

Yet during more than half the time, there were few young men, or men in prime, in the streets of Rome. They were fighting more than half the year, while their fathers and their children stayed behind with the women. The women sat spinning and weaving wool in their little brown houses; the boys played, fought, ran races naked in the streets; the small girls had their quiet games and, surely, their dolls, made of rags, stuffed with the soft wool waste from their mothers' spindles and looms. The old men, scarred and seamed in the battles of an age when fighting was all hand to hand, kept the shops, or sunned themselves in the market-place, shelling and chewing lupins to pass the time, as the Romans have always done, and telling old tales, or boasting to each other of their half-grown grandchildren, and of their full-grown sons, fighting far away in the hills and the plains that Rome might have more possession. Meanwhile the maidens went in pairs to the springs to fetch water, or down to the river in small companies to wash the woollen clothes and dry them in the shade of the old wild trees, lest in the sun they should shrink and thicken; black-haired, black-eyed, dark-skinned maids, all of them, strong and light of foot, fit to be mothers of more soldiers, to slay more enemies, and bring back more spoil. Then, as in our own times, the flocks of goats were driven in from the pastures at early morning and milked from door to door, for each household, and driven out again to the grass before the sun was high. In the old wall there was the Cattle Gate, the Porta Mugonia, named, as the learned say, from the lowing of the herds. Then, as in the hill towns not long ago, the serving women, who were slaves, sat cross-legged on the ground in the narrow court within the house, with the hand-mill of two stones between them, and ground the wheat to flour for the day's meal. There have been wonderful survivals of the first age even to our own time.

But that which has not come down to us is the huge vitality of those men and women. The world's holders have never risen suddenly in hordes; they have always grown by degrees out of little nations, that could live through more than their neighbours. Calling up the vision of the first Rome, one must see, too, such human faces and figures of men as are hardly to be found among us nowadays,—the big features, the great, square, devouring jaws, the steadily bright eyes, the strongly built brows, coarse, shagged hair, big bones, iron muscles and starting sinews. There are savage countries that still breed such men. They may have11 their turn next, when we are worn out. Browning has made John the Smith a memorable type.

Rome was a clean city in those days. One of the Tarquins had built the great arched drain which still stands unshaken and in use, and smaller ones led to it, draining the Forum and all the low part of the town. The people were clean, far beyond our ordinary idea of them, as is plain enough from the contemptuous way in which the Latin authors use their strong words for uncleanliness. A dirty man was an object of pity, and men sometimes went about in soiled clothes to excite the public sympathy, as beggars do today in all countries. Dirt meant abject poverty, and in a grasping, getting race, poverty was the exception, even while simplicity was the rule. For all was simple with them, their dress, their homes, their lives, their motives, and if one could see the Rome of Tarquin the Proud, this simplicity would be of all characteristics the most striking, compared with what we know of later Rome, and with what we see about us in our own times. Simplicity is not strength, but the condition in which strength is least hampered in its full action.

It was easy to live simply in such a place and in such a climate, under a wise King. The check in the first straight run of Rome's history brought the Romans suddenly face to face with the first great complication of their career, which was the struggle between the rich and the poor; and again the half truth rises up to12 explain the fact. Men whose first instinct was to take and hold took from one another in peace when they could not take from their enemies in war, since they must needs be always taking from some one. So the few strong took all from the many weak, till the weak banded themselves together to resist the strong, and the struggle for life took a new direction.

The grim figure of Lucius Junius Brutus rises as the incarnation of that character which, at great times, made history, but in peace made trouble. The man who avenged Lucretia, who drove out the Tarquins, and founded the Republic, is most often remembered as the father who sat unmoved in judgment on his two traitor sons, and looked on with stony eyes while they paid the price of their treason in torment and death. That one deed stands out, and we forget how he himself fell fighting for Rome's freedom.

But still the evil grew at home, and the hideous law of creditor and debtor, which only fiercest avarice could have devised, ground the poor, who were obliged to borrow to pay the tax-gatherer, and made slaves of them almost to the ruin of the state.

Just then Etruria wakes, shadowy, half Greek, the central power of Italy, between Rome and Gaul. Porsena, the Lar of Clusium, comes against the city with a great host in gilded arms. Terror descends like a dark mist over the young nation. The rich fear for their riches, the poor for their lives. In haste the13 fathers gather great supplies of corn against a siege; credit and debt are forgotten; patrician and plebeian join hands as Porsena reaches Janiculum, and three heroic figures of romance stand forth from a host of heroes. Horatius keeps the bridge, first with two comrades, then, at the last, alone in the glory of single-handed fight against an army, sure of immortality whether he live or die. Scævola, sworn with the three hundred to slay the Lar, stabs the wrong man, and burns his hand to the wrist to show what tortures he can bear unmoved. Clœlia, the maiden hostage, rides her young steed at the yellow torrent, and swims the raging flood back to the Palatine. Clœlia and Horatius get statues in the Forum; Scævola is endowed with great lands, which his race holds for centuries, and leaves a name so great that two thousand years later, Sforza, greatest leader of the Middle Age, coveting long ancestry, makes himself descend from the man who burned off his own hand.

They are great figures, the two men and the noble girl, and real to us, in a way, because we can stand on the very ground they trod, where Horatius fought, where Scævola suffered and where Clœlia took the river. They are nearer to us than Romulus, nearer even than Lucretia, as each figure, following the city's quick life, has more of reality about it, and not less of heroism.

For two hundred years the Romans strove with each other in law making; the fathers for exclusive power14 and wealth, the plebeians for freedom, first, and then for office in the state; a time of fighting abroad for land, and of contention at home about its division. In fifty years the poor had their Tribunes, but it took them nearly three times as long, after that, to make themselves almost the fathers' equals in power.

Once they tried a new kind of government by a board of ten, and it held for a while, till again a woman's life turned the tide of Roman history, and fair young Virginia, stabbed by her father in the Forum, left a name as lasting as any of that day.

Romance again, but the true romance, above doubt, at last; not at all mythical, but full of fate's unanswerable logic, which makes dim stories clear to living eyes. You may see the actors in the Forum, where it all happened,—the lovely girl with frightened, wondering eyes; the father, desperate, white-lipped, shaking with the thing not yet done; Appius Claudius smiling among his friends and clients; the sullen crowd of strong plebeians, and the something in the chill autumn air that was a warning of fate and fateful change. Then the deed. A shriek at the edge of the throng; a long, thin knife, high in air, trembling before a thousand eyes; a harsh, heartbroken, vengeful voice; a confusion and a swaying of the multitude, and then the rising yell of men overlaid, ringing high in the air from the Capitol right across the Forum to the Palatine, and echoing back the doom of the Ten.

The deed is vivid still, and then there is sudden darkness. One thinks of how that man lived afterwards. Had Virginius a home, a wife, other children to mourn the dead one? Or was he a lonely man, ten times alone after that day, with the memory of one flashing moment always undimmed in a bright horror? Who knows? Did anyone care? Rome's story changed its course, turning aside at the river of Virginia's blood, and going on swiftly in another way.

To defeat this time, straight to Rome's first and greatest humiliation; to the coming of the Gauls, sweeping everything before them, Etruscans, Italians, Romans, up to the gates of the city and over the great moat and wall of Servius, burning, destroying, killing everything, to the foot of the central rock; baffled at the last stronghold on a dark night by a flock of cackling geese, but not caring for so small a thing when they had swallowed up the rest, or not liking the Latin land, perhaps, and so, taking ransom for peace and marching away northwards again through the starved and harried hills and valleys of Etruria to their own country. And six centuries passed away before an enemy entered Rome again.

But the Gauls left wreck and ruin and scarcely one stone upon another in the great desolation; they swept away all records of history, then and there, and the general destruction was absolute, so that the Rome of the Republic and of the Empire, the centre and capital16 of the world, began to exist from that day. Unwillingly the people bore back Juno's image from Veii, where they had taken refuge and would have stayed, and built houses, and would have called that place Rome. But the nobles had their own way, and the great construction began, of which there was to be no end for many hundreds of years, in peace and war, mostly while hard fighting was going on abroad.

ETRUSCAN BRIDGE AT VEII ETRUSCAN BRIDGE AT VEII

They built hurriedly at first, for shelter, and as best they could, crowding their little houses in narrow streets with small care for symmetry or adornment. The second Rome must have seemed but a poor village compared with the solidly built city which the Gauls had burnt, and it was long before the present could compare with the past. In haste men seized on fragments of all sorts, blocks of stone, cracked and defaced17 in the flames, charred beams that could still serve, a door here, a window there, and such bits of metal as they could pick up. An irregular, crowded town sprang up, and a few rough temples, no doubt as pied and meanly pieced as many of those early churches built of odds and ends of ruin, which stand to this day.

It is not impossible that the motley character of Rome, of which all writers speak in one way or another, had its first cause in that second building of the city. Rome without ruins would hardly seem Rome at all, and all was ruined in that first inroad of the savage Gauls,—houses, temples, public places. When the Romans came back from Veii they must have found the Forum not altogether unlike what it is today, but blackened with smoke, half choked with mouldering humanity, strewn with charred timbers, broken roof tiles and the wreck of much household furniture; a sorrowful confusion reeking with vapours of death, and pestilential with decay. It was no wonder that the poor plebeians lost heart and would have chosen to go back to the clear streets and cleaner air of Veii. Their little houses were lost and untraceable in the universal chaos. But the rich man's ruins stood out in bolder relief; he had his lands still; he still had slaves; he could rebuild his home; and he had his way.

But ever afterwards, though the Republic and the Empire spent the wealth of nations in beautifying the city, the trace of that first defeat remained. Dark and18 narrow lanes wound in and out, round the great public squares, and within earshot of the broad white streets, and the time-blackened houses of the poor stood huddled out of sight behind the palaces of the rich, making perpetual contrast of wealth and poverty, splendour and squalor, just as one may see today in Rome, in London, in Paris, in Constantinople, in all the mistress cities of the world that have long histories of triumph and defeat behind them.

The first Rome sprang from the ashes of the Alban volcano, the second Rome rose from the ashes of herself, as she has risen again and again since then. But the Gauls had done Rome a service, too. In crushing her to the earth, they had crushed many of her enemies out of existence; and when she stood up to face the world once more, she fought not to beat the Æquians or the Etruscans at her gates, but to conquer Italy. And by steady fighting she won it all, and brought home the spoils and divided the lands; here and there a battle lost, as in the bloody Caudine pass, but always more battles won, and more, and more, sternly relentless to revolt. Brutus had seen his own sons' heads fall at his own word; should Caius Pontius, the Samnite, be spared, because he was the bravest of the brave? To her faithful friends Rome was just, and now and then half-contemptuously generous.

The idle Greek fine gentlemen of Tarentum sat in their theatre one day, overlooking the sea, shaded[19] by dyed awnings from the afternoon sun, listening entranced to some grand play,—the Œdipus King, perhaps, or Alcestis, or Medea. Ten Roman trading ships came sailing round the point; and the wind failed, and they lay there with drooping sails, waiting for the land breeze that springs up at night. Perhaps some rough Latin sailor, as is the way today in calm weather when there is no work to be done, began to howl out one of those strange, endless songs which have been sung down to us, from ear to ear, out of the primeval Aryan darkness,—loud, long drawn out, exasperating in its unfinished cadence, jarring on the refined Greek ear, discordant with the actor's finely measured tones. In sudden rage at the noise —so it must have been—those delicate idlers sprang up and ran down to the harbour, and took the boats that lay there, and overwhelmed the unarmed Roman traders, slaying many of them. Foolish, cruel, almost comic. So a sensitive musician, driven half mad by a street organ, longs to rush out and break the thing to pieces, and kill the poor grinder for his barbarous noise.

But when there was blood in the harbour of Tarentum, and some of the ships had escaped on their oars, the Greeks were afraid; and when the message of war came swiftly down to them from inexorable Rome, their terror grew, and they sent to Pyrrhus of Epirus, who had set up to be a conqueror, to come and conquer Rome for the sake of certain æsthetic[20] fine gentlemen who could not bear to be disturbed at a good play on a spring afternoon. He came with all the pomp and splendour of Eastern warfare; he won a battle, and a battle, and half a battle, and then the Romans beat him at Beneventum, famous again and again, and utterly destroyed his army, and took back with them his gold and his jewels, and the tusks of his elephants, and the mastery of all Italy to boot, but not yet beyond dispute.

Creeping down into Sicily, Rome met Carthage, both giants in those days, and the greatest and last struggle began, with half the known world and all the known sea for a battle-ground. Round and round the Mediterranean, by water and land, they fought for a hundred and eighteen years, through four generations of men, as we should reckon it, both grasping and strong, both relentless, both sworn to win or perish for ever, both doing great deeds that are remembered still. The mere name of Regulus is a legion of legends in itself; the name of Hannibal is in itself a history, that of Fabius Maximus a lesson; and while history lasts, Cornelius Scipio and Scipio the African will not be forgotten. It is the story of many and terrible defeats, from each of which Rome rose, fiercely young, to win a dozen terrible little victories. It is strange that we remember the lost days best; misty Thrasymene and Cannæ's fearful slaughter rise first in the memory. Then all at once, within ten years, the scale turns, and Caius Claudius Nero hurls Hasdrubal's disfigured head high over ditch and palisade into his brother's camp, right to his brother's feet. And five years later, the battle of Zama, won almost at the gates of Carthage; and then, almost the end, as great heartbroken Hannibal, defeated, ruined and exiled, drinks up the poison and rests at last, some forty years after he led his first army to victory. But he had been dead nearly forty years, when another Scipio at last tore down the walls of Carthage, and utterly destroyed the city to the foundations, for ever. And a dozen years later than that, Rome had conquered all the civilized world round about the Mediterranean sea, from Spain to Asia.

II
TOMBS ON THE APPIAN WAY TOMBS ON THE APPIAN WAY

There was a mother in Rome, not rich, but of great race, for she was daughter to Scipio of Africa; and she called her sons her jewels when other women showed their golden ornaments and their precious stones and boasted of their husbands' wealth. Cornelia's two sons, Tiberius and Caius, lost their lives successively in a struggle against the avarice of the rich men who ruled Rome, Italy and the world; against that grasping avarice which far surpassed the greed of any other race before the Romans, or after them, and which had suddenly taken new growth as the spoils of the East and South and West poured into the city. Yet the vast booty men could see was but an earnest of the wide lands which had fallen to Rome, called 'Public Lands' almost as if in derision, while they fell into the power23 of the few and strong, by the hundred thousand acres at a time.

Three hundred and fifty years before the Gracchi, when little conquests still seemed great, Spurius Cassius had died in defence of his Agrarian Law, at the hands of the savage rich who accused him of conspiring for a crown. Tiberius Gracchus set up the rights of the people to the public land, and perished.

He fell within a stone's throw of the spot on which the great tribune, Nicholas Rienzi, died. The strong, small band of nobles, armed with staves and clubs, and with that supremacy of contemptuous bearing that cows the simple, plough their way through the rioting throng, murderously clubbing to right and left. Tiberius, retreating, stumbles against a corpse and his enemies are upon him; a stave swung high in air, a dull blow, and all is finished for that day, save to throw the body into the Tiber lest the people should make a revolution of its funeral.

Next came Caius, a boy of six and twenty, fighting the same fight for a few years. On his head the nobles set a price—its weight in gold. He hides on the Aventine, and the Aventine is stormed. He escapes by the Sublician bridge and the bridge is held behind him by one friend, almost as Horatius held it against an army. Yet the nobles and their hired Cretan bowmen force the way and pursue him into Furina's grove. There a Greek slave ends him, and to get more gold24 fills the poor head with metal—and is paid in full. Three hundred died with Tiberius, three thousand were put to death for his brother's sake. With the goods of the slain and the dowries of their wives, Opimius built the Temple of Concord on the spot where the later one still stands in part, between the Comitium and the Capitol. The poor of Rome, and Cornelia, and the widows and children of the murdered men, knew what that 'Concord' meant.

BRASS OF TIBERIUS, SHOWING THE TEMPLE OF CONCORD
BRASS OF TIBERIUS, SHOWING THE TEMPLE OF CONCORD

Then followed revolution, war with runaway slaves, war with the immediate allies, then civil war, while wealth and love of wealth grew side by side, the one, insatiate, devouring the other.

First the slaves made for Sicily, wild, mountainous, half-governed then as it is today, and they held much of it against their masters for five years. Within short memory, almost yesterday, a handful of outlaws has defied a powerful nation's best soldiers in the same mountains. It is small wonder that many thousand men, fighting for liberty and life, should have held out so long.

And meanwhile Jugurtha of Numidia had for long years bought every Roman general sent against him, had come to Rome himself and bought the laws, and had gone back to his country with contemptuous leave-taking—'Thou city where all is sold!' And still he bought, till Caius Marius, high-hearted plebeian and great soldier, brought him back to die in the Mamertine prison.

Then against wealth arose the last and greatest power of Rome, her terrible armies that set up whom they would, to have their will of Senate and fathers and people. First Marius, then Sylla whom he had taught to fight, and taught to beat him in the end, after Cinna had been murdered for his sake at Ancona.

Marius and Sylla, the plebeian and the patrician, were matched at first as leader and lieutenant, then both as conquerors, then as alternate despots of Rome and mortal foes, till their long duel wrecked what had been and opened ways for what was to be.

First, Sylla claims that he, and not Marius, took Jugurtha, when the Numidian ally betrayed him, though the King and his two sons marched in the train of the plebeian's triumph. Marius answers by a stupendous victory over the Cimbrians and Teutons, slays a hundred thousand in one battle, comes home, triumphs again, sets up his trophies in the city and builds a temple to Honour and Courage. Next, in greed of popular power, he perjures himself to support a pair of murderous demagogues, betrays them in turn to the patricians, and

Saturninus is pounded to death with 26 roof tiles in the Capitol. Then, being made leader in the war with the allies, already old for fighting, he fails at the outset, and his rival Sylla is General in his stead.

Then riot on riot in the Forum, violence after violence in the struggle for the consulship, murder after murder, blood upon blood not yet dry. Sylla gets the expedition against Mithridates; Marius, at home, undermines his enemy's influence and forces the tribes to give him the command, and sends out his lieutenants to the East. Sylla's soldiers murder them, and Sylla marches back against Rome with six legions. Marius is unprepared; Sylla breaks into the city, torch in hand, at the head of his troops, burning and slaying; the rivals meet face to face in the Esquiline market-place, Roman fights Roman, and the plebeian loses the day and escapes to the sea.

The reign of terror begins, and a great slaying. Sylla declares his rival an enemy of Rome, and Marius is found hiding in the marshes of Minturnæ, is dragged out naked, covered with mud, a rope about his neck, and led into a little house of the town to be slain by a slave. 'Darest thou kill Caius Marius?' asks the old man with flashing eyes, and the slave executioner trembles before the unarmed prisoner. They let him go. He wanders to Africa and sits alone among the ruins of Carthage, while Sylla fights victoriously in the East. Rome, momentarily free of both, is torn by 27 dissensions about the voting of the newly enfranchised. Instead of the greater rivals, Cinna and Octavius are matched for plebs and nobles. Knife-armed the parties fight it out in the Forum, the bodies of citizens lie in heaps, and the gutters are gorged with free blood, and again the patricians win the day. Cinna, fleeing from wrath, is deposed from office. Marius sees his chance again. Unshaven and unshorn since he left Rome last, he joins Cinna, leading six thousand fugitives, seizes and plunders the towns about Rome, while Cinna encamps beneath the walls. Together they enter Rome and nail Octavius' head to the Rostra. Then the vengeance of wholesale slaying, in another reign of terror, and Marius is despot of the city for a while, as Sylla had been before, till spent with age, his life goes out amid drunkenness and blood. The people tear down Sylla's house, burn his villa and drive out his wife and his children. Back he comes after four years, victorious, fighting his way right and left, against Lucanians and Samnites, back to Rome still fighting them, almost loses the battle, is saved by Crassus to take vengeance again, and again the long lists of the proscribed are written out and hung up in the Forum, and the city runs blood in a third Terror. Amid heaps of severed heads, Sylla sits before the temple of Castor and sells the lands of his dead enemies; and Catiline is first known to history as the executioner of Caius Gratidianus, whom he slices to death, piecemeal, beyond the Tiber.

THE TARPEIAN ROCK

Sylla, cold, aristocratic, sublimely ironical monster, was Rome's first absolute and undisputed military lord. Tired of blood, he tried reform, invented an aristocratic constitution, saw that it must fail, and then, to the amazement of his friends and enemies, abdicated and withdrew to private life, protected by a hundred thousand veterans of his army, and many thousands of freedmen, to die at the last without violence.

Of the chaos he left behind him, Cæsar made the Roman Empire.

The Gracchi, champions of the people, were foully done to death. Marius and Sylla, tearing the proud Republic to pieces for their own greatness, both died in their beds, the one of old age, the other of disease. There is no irony like that which often ended the lives of great Romans. Marcus Manlius, who saved the Capitol from the Gauls, was hurled to his death from the same rock, by the tribunes of the people, and Rome's citadel and sanctuary was desecrated by the blood of its preserver. Scipio of Africa breathed his last in exile, but Appius Claudius, the Decemvir, died rich and honoured.

One asks, naturally enough, how Rome could hold the civilized nations in subjection while she was fighting out a civil war that lasted fifty years. We have but little idea of her great military organization, after arms became a profession and a career. We can but call up scattered pictures to show us rags and fragments of the immense host that patrolled the world with measured tread and matchless precision of serried rank, in tens and scores and hundreds of thousands, for centuries, shoulder to shoulder and flank to flank, learning its own strength by degrees, till it suddenly grasped all power, gave it to one man, and made Caius Julius Cæsar Dictator of the earth.

The greatest figure in all history suddenly springs out30 of the dim chaos and shines in undying glory, the figure of a man so great that the office he held means Empire, and the mere name he bore means Emperor today in four empires,—Cæsar, Kaiser, Czar, Kaisár,—a man of so vast power that the history of humanity for centuries after him was the history of those who were chosen to fill his place—the history of nearly half the twelve centuries foretold by the augur Attus, from Romulus, first King, to Romulus Augustulus, last Emperor. He was a man whose deeds and laws have marked out the life of the world even to this far day. Before him and with him comes Pompey, with him and after him Mark Antony, next to him in line and greatness, Augustus—all dwarfs compared with him, while two of them were failures outright, and the third could never have reached power but in his steps.

PALACE OF THE CÆSARS

In that long tempest of parties wherein the Republic went down for ever, it is hard to trace the truth, or number the slain, or reckon up account of gain and loss. But when Cæsar rises in the centre of the storm the end is sure and there can be no other, for he drives it before him like a captive whirlwind, to do his bidding and clear the earth for his coming. Other men, and great men, too, are overwhelmed by it, dashed down and stunned out of all sense and judgment, to be lost and forgotten like leaves in autumn, whirled away before the gale. Pompey, great general and great statesman, conqueror in Spain, subduer of Spartacus and the Gladiators, destroyer of pirates and final victor over Mithridates, comes back and lives as a simple citizen. Noble of birth, but not trusted by his peers, he joins with Cæsar, leader of all the people, and with Crassus, for more power, and loses the world by giving Cæsar an army, and Gaul to conquer. Crassus, brave general, too, is slain in battle in far Parthia, and Pompey steals a march by getting a long term in Spain. Cæsar demands as much and is refused by Pompey's friends. Then the storm breaks and Cæsar comes back from Gaul to cross the Rubicon, and take all Italy in sixty days. Pompey, ambitious, ill-starred, fights losing battles everywhere. Murdered at last in Egypt, he, too, is dead, and Cæsar stands alone, master of Rome and of the world. One year he ruled, and then they slew him; but no one of them that struck him died a natural death.

Creation presupposes chaos, and it is the divine prerogative of genius to evolve order from confusion. Julius Cæsar found the world of his day consisting of disordered elements of strength, all at strife with each other in a central turmoil, skirted and surrounded by the relative peace of an ancient and long undisturbed barbarism.

It was out of these elements that he created what has become modern Europe, and the direction which he gave to the evolution of mankind has never wholly changed since his day. Of all great conquerors he was the least cruel, for he never sacrificed human life without32 the direct intention of benefiting mankind by an increased social stability. Of all great lawgivers, he was the most wise and just, and the truths he set down in the Julian Code are the foundation of modern justice. Of all great men who have leaped upon the world as upon an unbroken horse, who have guided it with relentless hands, and ridden it breathless to the goal of glory, Cæsar is the only one who turned the race into the track of civilization and, dying, left mankind a future in the memory of his past. He is the one great man of all, without whom it is impossible to imagine history. We cannot take him away and yet leave anything of what we have. The world could have been as it is without Alexander, without Charlemagne, without Napoleon; it could not have been the world we know without Caius Julius Cæsar.

That fact alone places him at the head of mankind.

In Cæsar's life there is the same matter for astonishment as in Napoleon's; there is the vast disproportion between beginnings and climax, between the relative modesty of early aims and the stupendous magnitude of the climacteric result. One asks how in a few years the impecunious son of the Corsican notary became the world's despot, and how the fashionable young spendthrift lawyer of Rome, dabbling in politics and almost ignorant of warfare, rose in a quarter of a century to be the world's conqueror, lawgiver and civilizer. The daily miracle of genius is the incalculable33 speed at which it simultaneously thinks and acts. Nothing is so logical as creation, and creation is the first sign as well as the only proof that genius is present.

Hitherto the life of Cæsar has not been logically presented. His youth appears almost always to be totally disconnected from his maturity. The first success, the conquest of Gaul, comes as a surprise, because its preparation is not described. After it everything seems natural, and conquest follows victory as daylight follows dawn; but when we try to think backwards from that first expedition, we either see nothing clearly, or we find Cæsar an insignificant unit in a general disorder, as hard to identify as an individual ant in a swarming ant-hill. In the lives of all 'great men,' which are almost always totally unlike the lives of the so-called 'great,'—those born, not to power, but in power,—there is a point which must inevitably be enigmatical. It may be called the Hour of Fate—the time when in the suddenly loosed play of many circumstances, strained like springs and held back upon themselves, a man who has been known to a few thousands finds himself the chief of millions and the despot of a nation.

Things which are only steps to great men are magnified to attainments in ordinary lives, and remembered with pride. The man of genius is sure of the great result, if he can but get a fulcrum for his lever. What strikes one most in the careers of such men as Cæsar and Napoleon is the tremendous34 advance realized at the first step—the difference between Napoleon's half-subordinate position before the first campaign in Italy and his dominion of France immediately after it, or the distance which separated Cæsar, the impeached Consul, from Cæsar, the conqueror of Gaul.

It must not be forgotten that Cæsar came of a family that had held great positions, and which, though impoverished, still had credit, subsequently stretched by Cæsar to the extreme limit of its borrowing power. At sixteen, an age when Bonaparte was still an unknown student, Cæsar was Flamen Dialis, or high priest of Jupiter, and at one and twenty, the 'ill-girt boy,' as Sylla called him from his way of wearing his toga, was important enough to be driven from Rome, a fugitive. His first attempt at a larger notoriety had failed, and

Dolabella, whom he had impeached, had been acquitted through the influence of friends. Yet the young lawyer had found the opportunity of showing what he could do, and it was not without reason that Sylla said of him, 'You will find many a Marius in this one Cæsar.'

Twenty years passed before the prophecy began to be realized with the commencement of Cæsar's career in Gaul, and more than once during that time his life seemed a failure in his own eyes, and he said scornfully and sadly of himself that he had done nothing to be remembered at an age when Alexander had already conquered the world.

Those twenty years which, to the thoughtful man, are by far the most interesting of all, appear in history as a confused and shapeless medley of political, military and forensic activity, strongly coloured by social scandals, which rested upon a foundation of truth, and darkened by accusations of worse kind, for which there is no sort of evidence, and which may be safely attributed to the jealousy of unscrupulous adversaries.

The first account of him, which we have in the seventeenth year of his age, evokes a picture of youthful beauty. The boy who is to win the world is appointed high priest of Jove in Rome,—by what strong influence we know not,—and we fancy the splendid youth with his tall figure, full of elastic endurance, the brilliant face, the piercing, bold, black eyes; we see him with the small mitre set back upon the dark and curling locks that grow low on the forehead, as hair often does that is to fall early, clad in the purple robe of his high office, summoning all his young dignity to lend importance to his youthful grace as he moves up to Jove's high altar to perform his first solemn sacrifice with his young consort; for the high priesthood of Jove was held jointly by man and wife, and if the wife died the husband lost his office.

He was about twenty when he cast his lot with the people, and within the year he fled from Sylla's persecution. The life of sudden changes and contrasts had begun. Straight from the sacred office, with all36 its pomp, and splendour, and solemnity, Cæsar is a fugitive in the Sabine hills, homeless, wifeless, fever-stricken, a price on his head. Such quick chances of evil fell to many in the days of the great struggle between Marius and Sylla, between the people and the nobles.

Then as Sylla yielded to the insistence of the young 'populist' nobleman's many friends, the quick reverse is turned to us. Cæsar has a military command, sees some fighting and much idleness by the shores of the Bosphorus, in Bithynia—then in a fit of sudden energy, the soldier's spirit rises; he dashes to the attack on Mytilene, and shows himself a man.

CAIUS JULIUS CÆSAR CAIUS JULIUS CÆSAR

After a statue in the Palazzo dei Conservatori

One or two unimportant campaigns, as a subordinate officer, a civic crown won for personal bravery, an unsuccessful action brought against a citizen of high rank in the hope of forcing himself into notice, a trip to Rhodes made to escape the disgrace of failure, and37 an adventure with pirates—there, in a few words, is the story of Julius Cæsar's youth, as history tells it. But then suddenly, when his projected studies in quiet Rhodes were hardly begun, he crosses to the mainland, raises troops, seizes cities, drives Mithridates' governor out of the province, returns to Rome and is elected military tribune. The change is too quick, and one does not understand it. Truth should tell that those early years had been spent in the profound study of philosophy, history, biography, languages and mankind, of the genesis of events from the germ to the branching tree, of that chemistry of fate which brews effect out of cause, and distils the imperishable essence of glory from the rougher liquor of vulgar success.

What strikes one most in the lives of the very great is that every action has a cumulative force beyond what it ever has in the existence of ordinary men. Success moves onward, passing through events on the same plane, as it were, and often losing brilliancy till it fades away, leaving those who have had it to outlive it in sorrow and weakness. Genius moves upward, treading events under its feet, scaling Olympus, making a ladder of mankind, outlasting its own activity for ever in a final and fixed glory more splendid than its own bright path. The really great man gathers power in action, the average successful man expends it.

And so it must be understood that Cæsar, in his early youth, was not wasting his gifts in what seemed to be a38 half-voluptuous, half-adventurous, wholly careless life, but was accumulating strength by absorbing into himself the forces with which he came in contact, exhausting the intelligence of his companions in order to stock his own, learning everything simultaneously, forgetting nothing he learned till he could use all he knew to the extreme limit of its value.

There is something mysterious in the almost unlimited credit which Cæsar seems to have enjoyed when still a very young man; and if the control of enormous sums of money by which he made himself beloved among the people explains, in a measure, his rapid rise from office to office, it is, on the other hand, hard to account for the trust which his creditors placed in his promises, and to explain why, when he was taken by pirates, the cities of Asia Minor should have voluntarily contributed money to make up the ransom demanded, seeing that he had never served in Asia, except as a subordinate.

The only possible explanation is that while there, his real energies were devoted to the attainment of the greatest possible popularity in the shortest possible time, and that he was making himself beloved by the Asiatic cities, while his enemies said of him that he was wasting his time in idleness and dissipation.

In any case, it was the control of money that most helped him in obtaining high offices in Rome, and from the very first he seems to have acted on the principle that in great enterprises economy spells ruin, and that39 to check expenditure is to trip up success. And this is explained, if not justified, by his close association with the people, from his very childhood. Until he was made Pontifex Maximus he seems to have lived in a small house in the Suburra, in one of the most crowded and least fashionable quarters of Rome; and as a mere boy, it was his influence with the common people that roused Sylla's anxiety. To live with the people, to take their part against the nobles, to give them of all he had and of all he could borrow, were the chief rules of his conduct, and the fact that he obtained such enormous loans proves that there were rich lenders who were ready to risk fortunes upon his success. And it was in dealing with the Roman plebeian that he learned to command the Roman soldier, with the tact of a demagogue and the firmness of an autocrat. He knew that a man must give largely, even recklessly, to be beloved, and that in order to be respected he must be able to refuse coldly and without condition, and that in all ages the people are but as little children before genius, though they may rise against talent like wild beasts and tear it to death.

He knew also that in youth ten failures are nothing compared with one success, while in the full meridian of power one failure undoes a score of victories; hence his recklessness at first, his magnificent caution in his latter days; his daring resistance of Sylla's power before he was twenty, and his mildness towards the40 ringleaders of popular conspiracies against him when he was near his end; his violence upon the son of King Juba, whom he seized by the beard in open court when he himself was but a young lawyer, and his moderation in bearing the most atrocious libels, to punish which might have only increased their force.

Cæsar's career divides itself not unnaturally into three periods, corresponding with his youth, his manhood and his maturity; with the absorption of force in gaining experience, the lavish expenditure of force in conquest, the calm employment of force in final supremacy. The man who never lost a battle in which he commanded in person, began life by failing in everything he attempted, and ended it as the foremost man of all humanity, past and to come, the greatest general, the greatest speaker, the greatest lawgiver, the greatest writer of Latin prose whom the great Roman people ever produced, and also the bravest man of his day, as he was the kindest. In an age when torture was a legitimate part of justice, he caused the pirates who had taken him, and whom he took in turn, to be mercifully put to death before he crucified their dead bodies for his oath's sake, and when his long-trusted servant tried to poison him he would not allow the wretch to be hurt save by the sudden stroke of instant death; nor ever in a long career of conquest did he inflict unnecessary pain. Never was man loved of women as he was, and his sins were many even for those days, yet in them we find no unkindness, and when his own wife should have been condemned for her love of Clodius, Cæsar would not testify against her. He divorced her, he said, not because he knew anything, but because his family should be above suspicion. He plundered the world, but he gave it back its gold in splendid gifts and public works, keeping its glory alone for himself. He was hated by the few because he was beloved by the many, and it was not revenge, but envy, that slew the benefactor of mankind. The weaknesses of the supreme conqueror were love of woman and trust of man, and as the first Brutus made his name glorious by setting his people free, the second disgraced it and blackened the name of friendship with a stain that will outlast time, and by a deed second only in infamy to that of Judas Iscariot. The last cry of the murdered master was the cry of a broken heart—'And thou, too, Brutus, my son!' Alexander left chaos behind him; Cæsar left Europe, and it may be truly said that the crowning manifestation of his sublime wisdom was his choice of Octavius—of the young Augustus—to complete the carving of a world which he himself had sketched and blocked out in the rough.

The first period of his life ended with his election to the military tribuneship on his return to Rome after his Asian adventures, and his first acts were directed towards the reconstruction of what Sylla had destroyed, by reëstablishing the authority of tribunes and recalling some of Sylla's victims from their political exile. From that time onward, in his second period, he was more or less continually in office. Successively a tribune, a quæstor, governor of Farther Spain, ædile, pontifex maximus, prætor, governor of Spain again, and consul with the insignificant Bibulus, a man of so small importance that people used to date documents, by way of a jest, 'in the Consulship of Julius and Cæsar.' Then he obtained Gaul for his province, and lived the life of a soldier for nine years, during which he created the army that gave him at last the mastery of Rome. And in the tenth year Rome was afraid, and his enemies tried to deprive him of his power and passed bills against him, and drove out the tribunes of the people who took his part; and if he had returned to Rome then, yielding up his province and his legions, as he was called upon to do, he would have been judged and destroyed by his enemies. But he knew that the people loved him, and he crossed the Rubicon in arms.

This second period of his life closed with the last triumph decreed to him for his victories in Spain. The third and final period had covered but one year when his assassins cut it short.

Nothing demonstrates Cæsar's greatness so satisfactorily as this, that at his death Rome relapsed at43 once into civil war and strife as violent as that to which Cæsar had put an end, and that the man who brought lasting peace and unity into the distracted state, was the man of Cæsar's choice. But in endeavouring to realize his supreme wisdom, nothing helps us more than the pettiness of the accusations brought against him by such historians as Suetonius—that he once remained seated to receive the whole body of Conscript fathers, that he had a gilded chair in the Senate house, and appointed magistrates at his own pleasure to hold office for terms of years, that he laughed at an unfavourable omen and made himself dictator for life; and such things, says the historian, 'are of so much more importance than all his good qualities that he is considered to have abused his power and to have been justly assassinated.' But it is the people, not the historian, who make history, and when Caius Julius Cæsar was dead, the people called him God.

Beardless Octavius, his sister's daughter's son, barely eighteen years old, brings in by force the golden age of Rome. As Triumvir, with Antony and Lepidus, he hunts down the murderers first, then his rebellious colleagues, and wins the Empire back in thirteen years. He rules long and well, and very simply, as commanding general of the army and by no other power, taking all into his hands besides, the Senate, the chief priesthood, and the Majesty of Rome over the whole earth, for which he was called Augustus, the 'Majestic.'44 And his strength lay in this, that by the army, he was master of Senate and people alike, so that they could no longer strive with each other in perpetual bloodshed, and the everlasting wars of Rome were fought against barbarians far away, while Rome at home was prosperous and calm and peaceful. Then Virgil sang, and Horace gave Latin life to Grecian verse, and smiled and laughed, and wept and dallied with love, while Livy wrote the story of greatness for us all to this day, and Ovid touched another note still unforgotten. Then temple rose by temple, and grand basilicas reared their height by the Sacred Way; the gold of the earth poured in and Art was queen and mistress of the age. Julius Cæsar was master in Rome for one year. Augustus ruled nearly half a century. Four and forty years he was sole monarch after Antony's fall at Actium. About the thirtieth year of his reign, Christ was born.

All men have an original claim to be judged by the standard of their own time. Counting one by one the victims of the proscription proclaimed by the triumvirate in which Augustus was the chief power, some historians have brought down his greatness in quick declination to the level of a cold-blooded and cruel selfishness; and they account for his subsequent just and merciful conduct on the ground that he foresaw political advantage in clemency, and extension of power in the exercise of justice. The death of Cicero, sacrificed 45 to Antony's not unreasonable vengeance, is magnified into a crime that belittles the Augustan age.

Yet compared with the wholesale murders done by Marius and Sylla, and by the patricians themselves in their struggles with the people, the few political executions ordered by Augustus sink into comparative insignificance, and it will generally be seen that those who most find fault with him are ready to extol the murderers of Julius Cæsar as devoted patriots, if not as glorious martyrs to the divine cause of liberty.

OCTAVIUS AUGUSTUS CÆSAR OCTAVIUS AUGUSTUS CÆSAR

After a bust in the British Museum

It is easier, perhaps, to describe the growth of Rome from the early Kings to Augustus, than to account for the change from the Rome of the Empire at the beginning of our era to the Rome of the Popes in the year eight hundred. Probably the easiest and truest way of looking at the transition is to regard it according to the periods of supremacy, decadence and ultimate disappearance from Rome of 46 the Roman Army. For the Army made the Emperors, and the Emperors made the times. The great military organization had in it the elements of long life, together with all sudden and terrible possibilities. The Army made Tiberius, Caligula, Claudius and Nero, the Julian Emperors; then destroyed Nero and set up Vespasian after one or two experiments. The Army chose such men as Trajan and Marcus Aurelius, and such monsters as Domitian and Commodus; the Army conquered the world, held the world and gave the world to whomsoever it pleased. The Army and the Emperor, each the other's tool, governed Rome for good and ill, for ill and good, by fear and bounty and largely by amusement, but ultimately to their own and Rome's destruction.

For all the time the two great adversaries of the Empire, the spiritual and material, the Christian and the men of the North, were gaining strength and unity. Under Augustus, Christ was born. Under Augustus, Hermann the German chieftain destroyed Varus and his legions. By sheer strength and endurance, the Army widened and broadened the Empire, forcing back the Northmen upon themselves like a spring that gathers force by tension. Unnoticed, at first, Christianity quietly grew to power. Between Christians and Northmen, the Empire of Rome went down at last, leaving the Empire of Constantinople behind it.

The great change was wrought in about five hundred years, by the Empire, from the City of the Republic to what had become the City of the Middle Age; between the reign of Augustus, first Emperor, and the deposition of the last Emperor, Romulus Augustulus, by Odoacer, Rome's hired Pomeranian general.

In that time Rome was transubstantiated in all its elements, in population, in language, in religion and in customs. To all intents and purposes, the original Latin race utterly disappeared, and the Latin tongue became the broken dialect of a mixed people, out of which the modern Italian speech was to grow, decadent in form, degenerate in strength but renascent in a grace and beauty which the Latin never possessed. First the vast population of slaves brought in their civilized and their barbarous words—Greek, Hebrew and Arabic, or Celtic, German and Slav; then came the Goth, and filled all Italy with himself and his rough language for a hundred years. The Latin of the Roman Mass is the Latin of slaves in Rome between the first and fifth centuries, from the time of the Apostles to that of Pope Gelasius, whose prayer for peace and rest is the last known addition to the Canon, according to most authorities. Compare it with the Latin of Livy and Tacitus; it is not the same language, for to read the one by no means implies an understanding of the other.

Or take the dress. It is told of Augustus, as a strange and almost unknown thing, that he wore breeches and stockings, or leg swathings, because he suffered continually with cold. Men went barelegged and wrapped themselves in the huge toga which came down to their feet. In the days of Augustulus the toga was almost forgotten; men wore leggings, tunics and the short Greek cloak.

In the change of religion, too, all customs were transformed, private and public, in a way impossible to realize today. The Roman household, with the father as absolute head, lord and despot, gradually gave way to a sort of half-patriarchal, half-religious family life, resembling the first in principle but absolutely different from it in details and result, and which, in a measure, has survived in Italy to the present time.

In the lives of men, the terror of one man, as each despot lost power, began to give way to the fear of half-defined institutions, of the distant government in Constantinople and of the Church as a secular power, till the time came when the title of Emperor raised a smile, whereas the name of the Pope—of the 'Father-Bishop'—was spoken with reverence by Christians and with respect even by unbelievers. The time came when the army that had made Emperors and unmade them at its pleasure became a mere band of foreign mercenaries, who fought for wages and plunder when they could be induced to fight for Rome at all.

So the change came. But in the long five hundred years of the Western Empire Rome had filled the world with the results of her own life and had founded modern Europe, from the Danube to England and from the Rhine to Gibraltar; so that when the tide set towards the south again, the Northmen brought back to Italy some of the spirit and some of the institutions which Rome had carried northwards to them in the days of conquest; and they came not altogether as strangers and barbarians, as the Huns had come, to ravage and destroy, and be themselves destroyed and scattered and forgotten, but, in a measure, as Europeans against Europeans, hoping to grasp the remnants of a civilized power. Theodoric tried to make a real kingdom, Totila and Teias fell fighting for one; the Franks established one in Gaul, and at last it was a Frank who gave the Empire life again, and conquests and laws, and was crowned by the Christian Pontifex Maximus in Rome when Julius Cæsar had been dead more than eight hundred years.

One of the greatest of the world's historians has told the story of the change, calling it the 'Decline and Fall of the Empire,' and describing it in some three thousand pages, of which scarcely one can be spared for the understanding of the whole. Thereby its magnitude may be gauged, but neither fairly judged nor accurately measured. The man who would grasp the whole meaning of Rome's name, must spend a lifetime50 in study and look forward to disappointment in the end. It was Ampère, I believe, who told a young student that he might get a superficial impression of the city in ten years, but that twenty would be necessary in order to know anything about it worthy to be written. And perhaps the largest part of the knowledge worth having lies in the change from the ancient capital of the Empire to the mediæval seat of ecclesiastic domination.

And, indeed, nothing in all history is more extraordinary than the rise of Rome's second power under the Popes. In the ordinary course of human events, great nations appear to have had but one life. When that was lived out, and when they had passed through the artistic period so often coincident with early decadence, they were either swept away, or they sank to the insignificance of mere commercial prosperity, thereafter deriving their fashions, arts, tastes, and in fact almost everything except their wealth, from nations far gone in decay.

THE CAMPAGNA THE CAMPAGNA

And Ruins of the Claudian Aqueduct

But in Rome it was otherwise. The growth of the faith which subjected the civilized world was a matter of first importance to civilization, and Rome was the centre of that growing. Moreover, that development and that faith had one head, chosen by election, and the headship itself became an object of the highest ambition, whereby the strength and genius of individuals and families were constantly called into activity, and both families and isolated individuals of foreign race were attracted to Rome. It was no small thing to hold the kings of the earth in spiritual subjection, to be the arbiter of the new Empire founded by Charlemagne, the director of the kingdoms built up in France and England, and, almost literally, the feudal lord over all other temporal powers. The force of a predominant idea gave Rome new life, vivifying new elements with the vitality of new ambitions. The theatre was the same. The actors and the play had changed. The world was no longer governed by one man as monarch; it was directed by one man, who was the chief personage in the vast and intricate feudal system by which strong men agreed to live, and to which they forced the weak to submit.

The Barons came into existence, and Rome was a city of fortresses and towers, as well as churches. Orsini and Colonna, Caetani and Vitelleschi, Savelli and Frangipani, fought with each other for centuries among ruins, built strongholds of the stones of temples, and burned the marble treasures of the world to make lime. And fiercely they held their own. Nicholas Rienzi wanders amid the deserted places, deciphers the broken inscriptions, gathers a little crowd of plebeians about him and tells them of ancient Rome, and of the rights of the people in old times. All at once he rises, a grand shadow of a Roman, a true tribune, brave, impulsive, eloquent. A little while52 longer and he is half mad with vanity and ambition, a public fool in a high place, decking himself in silks and satins, and ornaments of gold, and the angry nobles slay him on the steps of the Aracœli, as other nobles long ago slew Tiberius Gracchus, a greater and a better man, almost on the same spot.

Meanwhile the great schism of the Church rages, before and after Rienzi. The Empire and its Kingdoms join issue with each other and with the Barons for the lordship of Christendom; there are two Popes, waging war with nations on both sides, and Rome is reduced to a town of barely twenty thousand souls. Then comes Hildebrand, Pope Gregory the Seventh, friend of the Great Countess, humbler of the Emperor, a restorer of things, the Julius Cæsar of the Church, and from his day there is stability again, as Urban the Second follows, like an Augustus; Nicholas the Fifth, the next great Pontiff, comes in with the Renascence. Last of destroyers Charles, the wild Constable of Bourbon, marches in open rebellion against King, State and Church, friend to the Emperor, straight to his death at the walls, his work of destruction carried out to the terrible end by revengeful Spaniards who spare only the churches and the convents. Out of those ashes Rome rose again, for the last time, the Rome of Sixtus the Fifth, which is, substantially, the Rome we see today; less powerful in the world after that time, but more beautiful as she grew more peaceful53 by degrees; flourishing in a strange, motley way, like no other city in the world, as the Empire of the Hapsburgs and the Kingdoms of Europe learned to live apart from her, and she was concentrated again upon herself, still and always a factor among nations, and ever to be. But even in latter days, Napoleon could not do without her, and Francis the Second of Austria had to resign the Empire, in order that Pius the Seventh might call the self-crowned Corsican soldier, girt with Charlemagne's huge sword, the anointed Emperor of Christendom.

Once more a new idea gives life to fragments hewn in pieces and scattered in confusion. A dream of unity disturbs Italy's sleep. Never, in truth, in all history, has Italy been united save by violence. By the sword the Republic brought Latins, Samnites and Etruscans into subjection; by sheer strength she crushed the rebellion of the slaves and then forced the Italian allies to a second submission; by terror Marius and Sylla ruled Rome and Italy; and it was the overwhelming power of a paid army that held the Italians in check under the Empire, till they broke away from each other as soon as the pressure was removed, to live in separate kingdoms and principalities for thirteen or fourteen hundred years, from Romulus Augustulus—or at least from Justinian—to Victor Emmanuel, King of Italy, in whose veins ran not one drop of Italian blood.

One asks whence came the idea of unity which has54 had such power to move these Italians, in modern times. The answer is plain and simple. Unity is the word; the interpretation of it is the name of Rome. The desire is for all the romance and the legends and the visions of supreme greatness which no other name can ever call up. What will be called hereafter the madness of the Italian people took possession of them on the day when Rome was theirs to do with as they pleased. Their financial ruin had its origin at that moment, when they became masters of the legendary Mistress of the world. What the end will be, no one can foretell, but the Rome of old was not made great by dreams. Her walls were founded in blood, and her temples were built with the wealth of conquered nations, by captives and slaves of subject races.

The Rome we see today owes its mystery, its sadness and its charm to six and twenty centuries of history, mostly filled with battle, murder and sudden death, deeds horrible in that long-past present which we try to call up, but alternately grand, fascinating and touching now, as we shape our scant knowledge into visions and fill out our broken dreams with the stuff of fancy. In most men's minds, perhaps, the charm lies in that very confusion of suggestions, for few indeed know Rome so well as to divide clearly the truth from the legend in her composition. Such knowledge is perhaps altogether unattainable in any history; it is most surely so here, where city is built on city, monument upon monument, road upon road, from the heart of the soil upwards—the hardened lava left by many eruptions of life; where the tablets of Clio have been shattered again and again, where fire has eaten, and sword has hacked, and hammer has bruised ages of records out of existence, where even the race and type of humanity have changed and have been forgotten twice and three times over.

Therefore, unless one have half a lifetime to spend in patient study and deep research, it is better, if one come to Rome, to feel much than to try and know a little, for in much feeling there is more human truth than in that dangerous little knowledge which dulls the heart and hampers the clear instincts of natural thought. Let him who comes hither be satisfied with a little history and much legend, with rough warp of fact and rich woof of old-time fancy, and not look too closely for the perfect sum of all, where more than half the parts have perished for ever.

It matters not much whether we know the exact site of Virgil's Laurentum; it is more interesting to remember how Commodus, cruel, cowardly and selfish, fled thither from the great plague, caring not at all that his people perished by tens of thousands in the city, since he himself was safe, with the famous Galen to take care of him. We can leave the task of tracing the enclosures of Nero's golden house to learned archæologists, and let our imagination find wonder and delight in their accounts of its porticos three thousand feet long, its game park, its baths, its thousands of columns with their gilded capitals, and its walls encrusted with mother-of-pearl. And we may realize the depth of Rome's abhorrence for the dead tyrant, as we think of how Vespasian and his son Titus pulled down the enchanted palace for the people's sake, and built the Colosseum where the artificial lake had been, and their great baths on the very foundations of Nero's gorgeous dwelling.

BRASS OF TRAJAN, SHOWING THE CIRCUS MAXIMUS BRASS OF TRAJAN, SHOWING THE CIRCUS MAXIMUS BRASS OF ANTONINUS PIUS, IN HONOUR OF FAUSTINA, WITH REVERSE SHOWING VESTA BEARING THE PALLADIUM BRASS OF ANTONINUS PIUS, IN HONOUR OF FAUSTINA, WITH REVERSE SHOWING VESTA BEARING THE PALLADIUM

III

It is impossible to conceive of the Augustan age without Horace, nor to imagine a possible Horace without Greece and Greek influence. At the same time Horace is in many ways the prototype of the old-fashioned, cultivated, gifted, idle, sarcastic, middle-class Roman official, making the most of life on a small salary and the friendship of a great personage; praising poverty, but making the most of the good things that fell in his way; extolling pristine austerity of life and yielding with a smile to every agreeable temptation; painting the idyllic life of a small gentleman farmer as the highest state of happiness, but secretly preferring the town; prudently avoiding marriage, but far too human to care for an existence in which woman had no share; more sensible in theory than in practice, and more religious in58 manner than in heart; full of quaint superstitions, queer odds and ends of knowledge, amusing anecdotes and pictures of personal experience; the whole compound permeated with a sort of indolent sadness at the unfulfilled promises of younger years, in which there had been more of impulse than of ambition, and more of ambition than real strength. The early struggles for Italian unity left many such half-disappointed patriots, and many less fortunate in their subsequent lives than Horace.

Born in the far South, and the son of a freed slave, brought to Rome as a boy and carefully taught, then sent to Athens to study Greek, he was barely twenty years of age when he joined Brutus after Cæsar's death, was with him in Asia, and, in the lack of educated officers perhaps, found himself one day, still a mere boy, tribune of a Legion—or, as we should say, in command of a brigade of six thousand men, fighting for what he believed to be the liberty of Rome, in the disastrous battle of Philippi. Brutus being dead, the dream of glory ended, after the amnesty, in a scribe's office under one of the quæstors, and the would-be liberator of his country became a humble clerk in the Treasury, eking out his meagre salary with the sale of a few verses. Many an old soldier of Garibaldi's early republican dreams has ended in much the same way in our own times under the monarchy.

But Horace was born to other things. Chaucer was59 a clerk in the Custom House, and found time to be the father of English poetry. Horace's daily work did not hinder him from becoming a poet. His love of Greek, acquired in Athens and Asia Minor, and the natural bent of his mind made him the greatest imitator and adapter of foreign verses that ever lived; and his character, by its eminently Italian combination of prim respectability and elastic morality, gave him a two-sided view of men and things that has left us representations of life in three dimensions instead of the flat, though often violent, pictures which prejudice loves best to paint.

In his admiration of Greek poetry, Horace was not a discoverer; he was rather the highest expression of Rome's artistic want. If Scipio of Africa had never conquered the Carthaginians at Zama, he would be notable still as one of the first and most sincere lovers of Hellenic literature, and as one of the earliest imitators of Athenian manners. The great conqueror is remembered also as the first man in Rome who shaved every day, more than a hundred and fifty years before Horace's time. He was laughed at by some, despised by others and disliked by the majority for his cultivated tastes and his refined manners.

The Romans had most gifts excepting those we call creative. Instead of creating, therefore, Rome took her art whole, and by force, from the most artistic nation the world ever produced. Sculptors, architects, painters and even poets, such as there were, came captive to Rome in gangs, were sold at auction as slaves, and became the property of the rich, to work all their lives at their several arts for their master's pleasure; and the State rifled Greece and Asia, and even the Greek Italy of the south, and brought back the masterpieces of an age to adorn Rome's public places. The Roman was the engineer, the maker of roads, of aqueducts, of fortifications, the layer out of cities, and the planner of harbours. In a word, the Roman made the solid and practical foundation, and then set the Greek slave to beautify it. When he had watched the slave at work for a century or two, he occasionally attempted to imitate him. That was as far as Rome ever went in original art.

But her love of the beautiful, though often indiscriminating and lacking in taste, was profound and sincere. It does not appear that in all her conquests her armies ever wantonly destroyed beautiful things. On the contrary, her generals brought home all they could with uncommon care, and the consequence was that in Horace's day the public places of the city were vast open-air museums, and the great temples picture galleries of which we have not the like now in the whole world. And with those things came all the rest; the manners, the household life, the necessaries and the fancies of a conquering and already decadent nation, the thousands of slaves whose only duty was61 to amuse their owners and the public; the countless men and women and girls and boys, whose souls and bodies went to feed the corruption of the gorgeous capital, or to minister to its enormous luxuries; the companies of flute-players and dancing-girls, the sharp-tongued jesters, the coarse buffoons, the play-actors and the singers. And then, the endless small commerce of an idle and pleasure-seeking people, easily attracted by bright colours, new fashions and new toys; the drug-sellers and distillers of perfumes, the venders of Eastern silks and linens and lace, the barbers and hairdressers, the jewellers and tailors, the pastry cooks and makers of honey-sweetmeats; and everywhere the poor rabble of failures, like scum in the wake of a great ship; the beggars everywhere, and the pickpockets and the petty thieves. It is no wonder that Horace was fond of strolling in Rome.

In contrast, the great and wonderful things of the Augustan city stand out in high relief, above the varied crowd that fills the streets, with all the dignity that centuries of power can lend. To the tawdry is opposed the splendid, the Roman general in his chiselled corselet and dyed mantle faces the Greek actor in his tinsel; the band of painted, half-clad, bedizened dancing-girls falls back cowering in awestruck silence as the noble Vestal passes by, high-browed, white-robed, untainted, the incarnation of purity in an age of vice. And the old Senator in his white cloak with its broad purple[62] hem, his smooth-faced clients at his elbows, his silent slaves before him and behind, meets the low-chattering knot of Hebrew money-lenders, making the price of short loans for the day, and discussing the assets of a famous spendthrift, as their yellow-turbaned, bearded fathers had talked over the chances of Julius Cæsar when he was as yet but a fashionable young lawyer of doubtful fortune, with an unlimited gift of persuasion and an equally unbounded talent for amusement.

Between the contrasts lived men of such position as Horace occupied, but not many. For the great middle element of society is a growth of later centuries, and even Horace himself, as time went on, became attached to Mæcenas and then, more or less, to the person of the Emperor, by a process of natural attraction, just as his butt, Tigellius, gravitated to the common herd that mourned his death. The 'golden mean' of which Horace wrote was a mere expression, taught him, perhaps, by his father, a part of his stock of maxims. Where there were only great people on the one side, and a rabble on the other, the man of genius necessarily rose to the level of the high, by his own instinct and their liking. What was best of Greek was for them, what was worst was for the populace.

But the Greek was everywhere, with his keen weak face, his sly look and his skilful fingers. Scipio and Paulus Emilius had brought him, and he stayed in Rome till the Goth came, and afterwards. Greek[63] poetry, Greek philosophy, Greek sculpture, Greek painting, Greek music everywhere—to succeed at all in such society, Virgil and Horace and Ovid must needs make Greek of Latin, and bend the stiff syllables to Alcaics and Sapphics and Hexameters. The task looked easy enough, though it was within the powers of so very few. Thousands tried it, no doubt, when the three or four had set the fashion, and failed, as the second-rate fail, with some little brief success in their own day, turned into the total failure of complete disappearance when they had been dead awhile.

Supreme of them all, for his humanity, Horace remains. Epic Virgil, appealing to the traditions of a living race of nobles and to the carefully hidden, sober vanity of the world's absolute monarch, does not appeal to modern man. The twilight of the gods has long deepened into night, and Ovid's tales of them and their goddesses move us by their own beauty rather than by our sympathy for them, though we feel the tender touch of the exiled man whose life was more than half love, in the marvellous Letters of Heroes' Sweethearts—in the complaint of Briseïs to Achilles, in the passionately sad appeal of Hermione to Orestes. Whoever has not read these things does not know the extreme limit of man's understanding of woman. Yet Horace, with little or nothing of such tenderness, has outdone Ovid and Virgil in this later age.

He strolled through life, and all life was a play of64 which he became the easy-going but unforgetful critic. There was something good-natured even in his occasional outbursts of contempt and hatred for the things and the people he did not like. There was something at once caressing and good-humouredly sceptical in his way of addressing the gods, something charitable in his attacks on all that was ridiculous,—men, manners and fashions.

He strolled wherever he would, alone; in the market, looking at everything and asking the price of what he saw, of vegetables and grain and the like; in the Forum, or the Circus, at evening, when 'society' was dining, and the poor people and slaves thronged the open places for rest and air, and there he used to listen to the fortune-tellers, and among them, no doubt, was that old hag, Canidia, immortalized in the huge joke of his comic resentment. He goes home to sup on lupins and fritters and leeks,—or says so,—though his stomach abhorred garlic; and his three slaves—the fewest a man could have—wait on him as he lies before the clean white marble table, leaning on his elbow. He does not forget the household gods, and pours a few drops upon the cement floor in libation to them, out of the little earthen saucer filled from the slim-necked bottle of Campanian earthenware. Then to sleep, careless of getting up early or late, just as he might feel, to stay at home and read or write, or to wander about the city, or to play the favourite65 left-handed game of ball in the Campus Marius before his bath and his light midday meal.

With a little change here and there, it is the life of the idle middle-class Italian today, which will always be much the same, let the world wag and change as it will, with all its extravagances, its fashions and its madnesses. Now and then he exclaims that there is no average common sense left in the world, no half-way stopping-place between extremes. One man wears his tunic to his heels, another is girt up as if for a race; Rufillus smells of perfumery, Gargonius of anything but scent; and so on—and he cries out that when a fool tries to avoid a mistake he will run to any length in the opposite direction. And Horace had a most particular dislike for fools and bores, and has left us the most famous description of the latter ever set down by an accomplished observer.

By chance, he says, he was walking one morning along the Sacred Street with one slave behind him, thinking of some trifle and altogether absorbed in it, when a man whom he barely knew by name came up with him in a great hurry and grasped his hand. 'How do you do, sweet friend?' asks the Bore. 'Pretty well, as times go,' answers Horace, stopping politely for a moment; and then beginning to move on, he sees to his horror that the Bore walks by his side. 'Can I do anything for you?' asks the poet, still civil, but hinting that he prefers his own company. The Bore plunges into the important business of praising himself, with a frankness not yet forgotten in his species, and Horace tries to get rid of him, walking very fast, then very slowly, then turning to whisper a word to his slave, and in his anxiety he feels the perspiration breaking out all over him, while his Tormentor chatters on, as they skirt the splendid Julian Basilica, gleaming in the morning sun. Horace looks nervously and eagerly to right and left, hoping to catch sight of a friend and deliverer. Not a friendly face was in sight, and the Bore knew it, and was pitilessly frank. 'Oh, I know you would like to get away from me!' he exclaimed. 'I shall not let you go so easily! Where are you going?' 'Across the Tiber,' answered Horace, inventing a distant visit. 'I am going to see someone who lives far off, in Cæsar's gardens —a man you do not know. He is ill.' 'Very well,' said the other; 'I have nothing to do, and am far from lazy. I will go all the way with you.' Horace hung his head, as a poor little Italian donkey does when a heavy load is piled upon his back, for he was fairly caught, and he thought of the long road before him, and he had moreover the unpleasant consciousness that the Bore was laughing at his imaginary errand, since they were walking in a direction exactly opposite from the Tiber, and would have to go all the way round the Palatine by the Triumphal Road and the Circus Maximus and then67 cross by the Sublician bridge, instead of turning back towards the Velabrum, the Provision Market and the Bridge of Æmilius, which we have known and crossed as the Ponte Rotto, but of which only one arch is left now, in midstream.

PONTE ROTTO, NOW DESTROYED PONTE ROTTO, NOW DESTROYED

After an engraving made about
Then, pressing his advantage, the Bore began again. 'If I am any judge of myself,' he observed, 'you will make me one of your most intimate friends. I am sure nobody can write such good verses as fast as I can. As for my singing, I know it for a fact that Hermogenes is decidedly jealous of me!' 'Have you a mother, Sir?' asked Horace, gravely. 'Have you any relations to whom your safety is a matter of importance?' 'No,' answered the other, 'no one. I have buried them all!' 'Lucky people!' said the poet to himself, and he wished he were dead, too, at that moment, and68 he thought of all the deaths he might have died. It was evidently not written that he should die of poison nor in battle, nor of a cough, nor of the liver, nor even of gout. He was to be slowly talked to death by a bore. By this time they were before the temple of Castor and Pollux, where the great Twin Brethren bathed their horses at Juturna's

spring. The temple of Vesta was before them, and the Sacred Street turned at right angles to the left, crossing over between a row of shops on one side and the Julian Rostra on the other, to the Courts of Law. The Bore suddenly remembered that he was to appear in answer to an action on that very morning, and as it was already nine o'clock, he could not possibly walk all the way to Cæsar's gardens and be back before noon, and if he was late, he must forfeit his bail, and the suit would go against him by default. On the other hand, he had succeeded in catching the great poet alone, after a hundred fruitless attempts, and the action was not a very important one, after all. He stopped short. 'If you have the slightest regard for me,' he said, 'you will just go across with me to the Courts for a moment.' Horace looked at him curiously, seeing a chance of escape. 'You know where I am going,' he answered with a smile; 'and as for law, I do not know the first thing about it.' The Bore hesitated, considered what the loss of the suit must cost him, and what he might gain by pushing his acquaintance69 with the friend of Mæcenas and Augustus. 'I am not sure,' he said doubtfully, 'whether I had better give up your company, or my case,' 'My company, by all means!' cried Horace, with alacrity. 'No!' answered the other, looking at his victim thoughtfully, 'I think not!' And he began to move on again by the Nova Via towards the House of the Vestals. Having made up his mind to sacrifice his money, however, he lost no time before trying to get an equivalent for it. 'How do you stand with Mæcenas?' he asked suddenly, fixing his small eyes on Horace's weary profile, and without waiting for an answer he ran on to praise the great man. 'He is keen and sensible,' he continued, 'and has not many intimate friends. No one knows how to take advantage of luck as he does. You would find me a valuable ally, if you would introduce me. I believe you might drive everybody else out of the field—with my help, of course.' 'You are quite mistaken there!' answered Horace, rather indignantly. 'He is not at all that kind of man! There is not a house in Rome where any sort of intrigue would be more utterly useless!' 'Really, I can hardly believe it!' 'It is a fact, nevertheless,' retorted Horace, stoutly. 'Well,' said the Bore, 'if it is, I am of course all the more anxious to know such a man!' Horace smiled quietly. 'You have only to wish it, my dear Sir,' he answered, with the faintest modulation of polite irony in his tone. 'With such70 gifts at your command, you will certainly charm him. Why, the very reason of his keeping most people at arm's length is that he knows how easily he yields!' 'In that case, I will show you what I can do,' replied the Bore, delighted. 'I shall bribe the slaves; I will not give it up, if I am not received at first! I will bide my time and catch him in the street, and follow him about. One gets nothing in life without taking trouble!' As the man was chattering on, Horace's quick eyes caught sight of an old friend at last, coming towards him from the corner of the Triumphal Road, for they had already almost passed the Palatine. Aristius, sauntering along and enjoying the morning air, with a couple of slaves at his heels, saw Horace's trouble in a moment, for he knew the Bore well enough, and realized at once that if he delivered his friend, he himself would be the next victim. He was far too clever for that, and with a cold-blooded smile pretended not to understand Horace's signals of distress. 'I forget what it was you wished to speak about with me so particularly, my dear Aristius,' said the poet, in despair. 'It was something very important, was it not?' 'Yes,' answered the other, with another grin, 'I remember very well; but this is an unlucky day, and I shall choose another time. Today is the thirtieth Sabbath,' he continued, inventing a purely imaginary Hebrew feast, 'and you surely would not risk a Jew's curse for a few moments of conversation, would you?' 'I have no religion!' exclaimed Horace, eagerly. 'No superstition! Nothing!' 'But I have,' retorted Aristius, still smiling. 'My health is not good—perhaps you did not know? I will tell you about it some other time.' And he turned on his heel, with a laugh, leaving Horace to his awful fate. Even the sunshine looked black. But salvation came suddenly in the shape of the man who had brought the action against the Bore, and who, on his way to the Court, saw his adversary going off in the opposite direction. 'Coward! Villain!' yelled the man, springing forward and catching the poet's tormentor by his cloak. 'Where are you going now? You are witness, Sir, that I am in my right,' he added, turning to look for Horace. But Horace had disappeared in the crowd that had collected to see the quarrel, and his gods had saved him after all.

TEMPLE OF CASTOR AND POLLUX TEMPLE OF CASTOR AND POLLUX

A part of the life of the times is in the little story, and anyone may stroll today along the Sacred Street, past the Basilica and the sharp turn that leads to the block of old houses where the Court House stood, between St. Adrian's and San Lorenzo in Miranda. Anyone may see just how it happened, and many know exactly how Horace felt from the moment when the Bore buttonholed him at the corner of the Julian Basilica till his final deliverance near the corner of the Triumphal Road, which is now the Via di San Gregorio.

ATRIUM OF VESTA ATRIUM OF VESTA

There was much more resemblance to our modern life than one might think at first sight. Perhaps, after his timely escape, Horace turned back along the Sacred Street, followed by his single slave, and retraced his steps, past the temple of Vesta, the temple of Julius Cæsar, skirting the Roman Forum to the Golden Milestone at the foot of the ascent to the Capitol, from which landmark all the distances in the Roman Empire were reckoned, the very centre of the known world. Thence, perhaps, he turned up towards the Argiletum, with something of that instinct which takes a modern man of letters to his publisher's when he is in the neighbourhood. There the 'Brothers Sosii' had their publishing establishment, among many others of the same nature, and employed a great staff of copyists in preparing volumes for sale. All the year round the skilled scribes sat within in rows, with pen and ink, working at the manufacture of books. The Sosii Brothers were rich, and probably owned their workmen as slaves, both the writers and those who prepared the delicate materials, the wonderful ink, of which we have not the like today, the fine sheets of papyrus,—Pliny tells how they were sometimes too rough, and how they sometimes soaked up the ink like a cloth, as happens with our own paper, —and the carefully cut pens of Egyptian reed on which so much of the neatness in writing depended, though Cicero says somewhere that he could write with any pen he chanced to take up.

It was natural enough that Horace should look in to ask how his latest book was selling, or more probably his first, for he had written but a few Epodes and not many Satires at the time when he met the immortal Bore. Later in his life, his books were published in editions of a thousand, as is the modern custom in Paris, and were sold all over the Empire, like those of other famous authors. The Satires did him little credit, and probably brought him but little money at their first publication. It seems certain that they have come down to us through a single copy. The Greek form of the Odes pleased people better. Moreover, some of the early Satires made distinguished people shy of his acquaintance, and when he told the Bore that Mæcenas[74] was difficult of access he remembered that nine months had elapsed from the time of his own introduction to the great man until he had received the latter's first invitation to dinner. More than once he went almost too far in his attacks on men and things and then tried to remove the disagreeable impression he had produced, and wrote again of the same subject in a different spirit—notably when he attacked the works of the dead poet Lucilius and was afterwards obliged to explain himself.

No doubt he often idled away a whole morning at his publisher's, looking over new books of other authors, and very probably borrowing them to take home with him, because he was poor, and he assuredly must have talked over with the Sosii the impression produced on the public by his latest poems. He was undoubtedly a quæstor's scribe, but it is more than doubtful whether he ever went near the Treasury or did any kind of clerk's work. If he ever did, it is odd that he should never speak of it, nor take anecdotes from such an occupation and from the clerks with whom he must have been thrown, for he certainly used every other sort of social material in the Satires. Among the few allusions to anything of the kind in his works are his ridicule of the over-dressed prætor of the town of Fundi, who had been a government clerk in Rome, and in the same story, his jest at one of Mæcenas' parasites, a freedman, and nominally a Treasury clerk, as Horace had75 been. In another Satire, the clerks in a body wish him to be present at one of their meetings.

Perhaps what strikes one most in the study of Horace, which means the study of the Augustan age, is the vivid contrast between the man who composed the Carmen Sæculare, the sacred hymn sung on the Tenth anniversary of Augustus' accession to the imperial power, besides many odes that breathe a pristine reverence for the gods, and, on the other hand, the writer of satirical, playfully sceptical verses, who comments on the story of the incense melting without fire at the temple of Egnatia, with the famous and often-quoted 'Credat Judæus'! The original Romans had been a believing people, most careful in all ceremonies and observances, visiting anything like sacrilege with a cool ferocity worthy of the Christian religious wars in later days. Horace, at one time or another, laughs at almost every god and goddess in the heathen calendar, and publishes his jests, in editions of a thousand copies, with perfect indifference and complete immunity from censorship, while apparently bestowing a certain amount of care on household sacrifices and the like.

The fact is that the Romans were a religious people, whereas the Italians were not. It is a singular fact that Rome, when left long to herself, has always shown a tendency to become systematically devout, whereas most of the other Italian states have exhibited an equally strong inclination to a scepticism not unfrequently76 mixed with the grossest superstition. It must be left to more profound students of humanity to decide whether certain places have a permanent influence in one determined direction upon the successive races that inhabit them; but it is quite undeniably true that the Romans of all ages have tended to religion of some sort in the most marked manner. In Roman history there is a succession of religious epochs not to be found in the annals of any other city. First, the early faith of the Kings, interrupted by the irruption of Greek influences which began approximately with Scipio Africanus; next, the wild Bacchic worship that produced the secret orgies on the Aventine, the discovery of which led to a religious persecution and the execution of thousands of persons on religious grounds; then the worship of the Egyptian deities, brought over to Rome in a new fit of belief, and at the same time, or soon afterwards, the mysterious adoration of the Persian Mithras, a gross and ignorant form of mysticism which, nevertheless, took hold of the people, at a time when other religions were almost reduced to a matter of form.

Then, as all these many faiths lost vitality, Christianity arose, the terribly simple and earnest Christianity of the early centuries, sown first under the Cæsars, in Rome's secure days, developing to a power when Rome was left to herself by the transference of the Empire to the East, culminating for the first time in the crowning of Charlemagne, again in the Crusades, sinking under77 the revival of mythology and Hellenism during the Renascence, rising again, by slow degrees, to the extreme level of devotion under Pius the Ninth and the French protectorate, sinking suddenly with the movement of Italian unity, and the coming of the Italians in , then rising again, as we see it now, with undying energy, under Leo the Thirteenth, and showing itself in the building of new churches, in the magnificent restoration of old ones, and in the vast second growth of ecclesiastical institutions, which are once more turning Rome into a clerical city, now that she is again at peace with herself, under a constitutional monarchy, but threatened only too plainly by an impending anarchic revolution. It would be hard to find in the history of any other city a parallel to such periodical recurrences of religious domination. Nor, in times when belief has been at its lowest ebb, have outward religious practices anywhere continued to hold so important a place in men's lives as they have always held in Rome. Of all Rome's mad tyrants, Elagabalus alone dared to break into the temple of Vesta and carry out the sacred Palladium. During more than eleven hundred years, six Vestal Virgins guarded the sacred fire and the Holy Things of Rome, in peace and war, through kingdom, republic, revolution and empire. For fifteen hundred years since then, the bones of Saint Peter have been respected by the Emperors, by Goths, by Kings, revolutions and short-lived republics.

BRASS OF GORDIAN, SHOWING THE COLOSSEUM BRASS OF GORDIAN, SHOWING THE COLOSSEUM
IV

There was a surprising strength in those early institutions of which the fragmentary survival has made Rome what it is. Strongest of all, perhaps, was the patriarchal mode of life which the shepherds of Alba Longa brought with them when they fled from the volcano, and of which the most distinct traces remain to the present day, while its origin goes back to the original Aryan home. Upon that principle all the household life ultimately turned in Rome's greatest times. The Senators were Patres, conscript fathers, heads of strong houses; the Patricians were those who had known 'fathers,' that is, a known and noble descent. Horace called Senators simply 'Conscripts,' and the Roman nobles of today call themselves the 'Conscript' families. The chain of tradition is unbroken from Romulus to our own time, while everything else has changed in greater or less degree.

It is hard for Anglo-Saxons to believe that, for more than a thousand years, a Roman father possessed the absolute legal right to try, condemn and execute any of his children, without witnesses, in his own house and without consulting anyone. Yet nothing is more certain. 'From the most remote ages,' says Professor Lanciani, the highest existing authority, 'the power of a Roman father over his children, including those by adoption as well as by blood, was unlimited. A father might, without violating any law, scourge or imprison his son, or sell him for a slave, or put him to death, even after that son had risen to the highest honours in the state.' During the life of the father, a child, no matter of what age, could own no property independently, nor keep any private accounts, nor dispose of any little belongings, no matter how insignificant, without the father's consent, which was never anything more than an act of favour, and was revocable at any moment, without notice. If a son became a public magistrate, the power was suspended, but was again in force as soon as the period of office terminated. A man who had been Dictator of Rome became his father's slave and property again, as soon as his dictatorship ended.

But if the son married with his father's consent, he was partly free, and became a 'father' in his turn, and absolute despot of his own household. So, if a daughter married, she passed from her father's dominion[80] to that of her husband. A Priest of Jupiter for life was free. So was a Vestal Virgin. There was a complicated legal trick by which the father could liberate his son if he wished to do so for any reason, but he had no power to set any of his children free by a mere act of will, without legal formality. The bare fact that the men of a people should be not only trusted with such power, but that it should be forcibly thrust upon them, gives an idea of the Roman character, and it is natural enough that the condition of family life imposed by such laws should have had pronounced effects that may still be felt. As the Romans were a hardy race and long-lived, when they were not killed in battle, the majority of men were under the absolute control of their fathers till the age of forty or fifty years, unless they married with their parents' consent, in which case they advanced one step towards liberty, and at all events, could not be sold as slaves by their fathers, though they still had no right to buy or sell property nor to make a will.

There are few instances of the law being abused, even in the most ferocious times. Brutus had the right to execute his sons, who conspired for the Tarquins, without any public trial. He preferred the latter. Titus Manlius caused his son to be publicly beheaded for disobeying a military order in challenging an enemy to single combat, slaying him, and bringing back the spoils. He might have cut off his head in private, so[81] far as the law was concerned, for any reason whatsoever, great or small.

As for the condition of real slaves, it was not so bad in early times as it became later, but the master's power was absolute to inflict torture and death in any shape. In slave-owning communities, barbarity has always been, to some extent, restrained by the actual value of the humanity in question, and slaves were not as cheap in Rome as might be supposed. A perfectly ignorant labourer of sound body was worth from eighty to a hundred dollars of our money, which meant much more in those days, though in later times twice that sum was sometimes paid for a single fine fish. The money value of the slave was, nevertheless, always a sort of guarantee of safety to himself; but men who had right of life and death over their own children, and who occasionally exercised it, were probably not, as a rule, very considerate to creatures who were bought and sold like cattle. Nevertheless, the number of slaves who were freed and enriched by their masters is really surprising.

The point of all this, however, is that the head of a Roman family was, under protection of all laws and traditions, an absolute tyrant over his wife, his children, and his servants; and the Roman Senate was a chosen association of such tyrants. It is astonishing that they should have held so long to the forms of a republican government, and should never have completely lost their republican traditions.

In this household tyranny, existing side by side with certain general ideas of liberty and constitutional government, under the ultimate domination of the Emperors' despotism as introduced by Augustus, is to be found the keynote of Rome's subsequent social life. Without those things, the condition of society in the Middle Age would be inexplicable, and the feudal system could never have developed. The old Roman principle that 'order should have precedence over order, not man over man,' rules most of Europe at the present day, though in Rome and Italy it is now completely eclipsed by a form of government which can only be defined as a monarchic democracy.

The mere fact that under Augustus no man was eligible to the Senate who possessed less than a sum equal to a quarter of a million dollars, shows plainly enough what one of the most skilful despots who ever ruled mankind wisely, thought of the institution. It was intended to balance, by its solidity, the ever-unsettled instincts of the people, to prevent as far as possible the unwise passage of laws by popular acclamation, and, so to say, to regulate the pulse of the nation. It has been imitated, in one way or another, by all the nations we call civilized.

But the father of the family was in his own person the despot, the senate, the magistrate and the executive of the law; his wife, his children and his slaves represented the people, constantly and eternally in real83 or theoretical opposition, while he was protected by all the force of the most ferocious laws. A father could behead his son with impunity; but the son who killed his father was condemned to be all but beaten to death, and then to be sewn up in a leathern sack and drowned. The father could take everything from the son; but if the son took the smallest thing from his father he was a common thief and malefactor, and liable to be treated as one, at his father's pleasure. The conception of justice in Rome never rested upon any equality, but always upon the precedence of one order over another, from the highest to the lowest. There were orders even among the slaves, and one who had been allowed to save money out of his allowances could himself buy a slave to wait on him, if he chose.

Hence the immediate origin of European caste, of different degrees of nobility, of the relative standing of the liberal professions, of the mediæval guilds of artisans and tradesmen, and of the numerous subdivisions of the agricultural classes, of which traces survive all over Europe. The tendency to caste is essentially and originally Aryan, and will never be wholly eliminated from any branch of the Aryan race.

One may fairly compare the internal life of a great nation to a building which rises from its foundations story by story until the lower part can no longer carry the weight of the superstructure, and the first signs of weakness begin to show themselves in the oldest and84 lowest portion of the whole. Carefully repaired, when the weakness is noticed at all, it can bear a little more, and again a little, but at last the breaking strain is reached, the tall building totters, the highest pinnacles topple over, then the upper story collapses, and the end comes either in the crash of a great falling or, by degrees, in the irreparable ruin of ages. But when all is over, and wind and weather and time have swept away what they can, parts of the original foundation still stand up rough and heavy, on which a younger and smaller people must build their new dwelling, if they build at all.

The aptness of the simile is still more apparent when we confront the material constructions of a nation with the degree of the nation's development or decadence at the time when the work was done.

It is only by doing something of that sort that we can at all realize the connection between the settlement of the shepherds, the Rome of the Cæsars, and the desolate and scantily populated fighting ground of the Barons, upon which, with the Renascence, the city of the later Popes began to rise under Nicholas the Fifth. And lastly, without a little of such general knowledge it would be utterly impossible to call up, even faintly, the lives of Romans in successive ages. Read the earlier parts of Livy's histories and try to picture the pristine simplicity of those primeval times. Read Cæsar's Gallic War, the marvellously concise reports of85 the greatest man that ever lived, during ten years of his conquests. Read Horace, and attempt to see a little of what he describes in his good-natured, easy way. Read the correspondence of the younger Pliny when proconsul in Bithynia under Trajan, and follow the extraordinary details of administration which, with ten thousand others, the Spanish Emperor of Rome carried in his memory, and directed and decided. Take Petronius Arbiter's 'novel' next, the Satyricon, if you be not over-delicate in taste, and glance at the daily journal of a dissolute wretch wandering from one scene of incredible vice to another. And so on, through the later writers; and from among the vast annals of the industrious Muratori pick out bits of Roman life at different periods, and try to piece them together. At first sight it seems utterly impossible that one and the same people should have passed through such social changes and vicissitudes. Every educated man knows the main points through which the chain ran. Scholars have spent their lives in the attempt to restore even a few of the links and, for the most part, have lost their way in the dry quicksands that have swallowed up so much.

'I have raised a monument more enduring than bronze!' exclaimed Horace, in one of his rare moments of pardonable vanity. The expression meant much more then than it does now. The golden age of Rome was an age of brazen statues apparently destined to last as86 long as history. Yet the marble outlasted the gilded metal, and Horace's verse outlived both, and the names of the artists of that day are mostly forgotten, while his is a household word. In conquering races, literature has generally attained higher excellence than painting or sculpture, or architecture, for the arts are the expression of a people's tastes, often incomprehensible to men who live a thousand years later; but literature, if it expresses anything, either by poetry, history, or fiction, shows the feeling of humanity; and the human being, as such, changes very little in twenty or thirty centuries. Achilles, in his wrath at being robbed of the lovely Briseïs, brings the age of Troy nearer to most men in its living vitality than the matchless Hermes of Olympia can ever bring the century of Greece's supremacy. One line of Catullus makes his time more alive today than the huge mass of the Colosseum can ever make Titus seem. We see the great stones piled up to heaven, but we do not see the men who hewed them, and lifted them, and set them in place. The true poet gives us the real man, and after all, men are more important than stones. Yet the work of men's hands explains the working of men's hearts, telling us not what they felt, but how the feelings which ever belong to all men more particularly affected the actors at one time or another during the action of the world's long play. Little things sometimes tell the longest stories.

THE COLOSSEUM THE COLOSSEUM

Pliny, suffering from sore eyes, going about in a closed carriage, or lying in the darkened basement portico of his house, obliged to dictate his letters, and unable to read, sends his thanks—by dictation—to his friend and colleague, Cornutus, for a fowl sent him, and says that although he is half blind, his eyes are sharp enough to see that it is a very fat one. The touch of human nature makes the whole picture live. Horace, journeying to Brindisi, and trying to sleep a little on a canal boat, is kept awake by mosquitoes and croaking frogs, and by the long-drawn-out, tipsy singing of a drunken sailor, who at last turns off the towing mule to graze, and goes to sleep till daylight. It is easier to see all this than to call up88 one instant of a chariot race in the great circus, or one of the ten thousand fights in the Colosseum, wherein gladiators fought and died, and left no word of themselves.

Yet, without the setting, the play is imperfect, and we must have some of the one to understand the other. For human art is, in the first place, a progressive commentary on human nature, and again, in quick reaction, stimulates it with a suggestive force. Little as we really know of the imperial times, we cannot conceive of Rome without the Romans, nor of the Romans without Rome. They belonged together; when the seat of Empire became cosmopolitan, the great dominion began to be weakened; and when a homogeneous power dwelt in the city again, a new domination had its beginning, and was built up on the ruins of the old.

Napoleon is believed to have said that the object of art is to create and foster agreeable illusions. Admitting the general truth of the definition, it appears perfectly natural that since the Romans had little or no art of their own, they should have begun to import Greek art just when they did, after the successful issue of the Second Punic War. Up to that time the great struggle had lasted. When it was over, the rest was almost a foregone conclusion. Rome and Carthage had made a great part of the known world their fighting ground in the duel that lasted a hundred and eighteen years; and the known world was the portion of the89 victor. Spoil first, for spoil's sake, he brought home; then spoil for the sake of art; then art for what itself could give him. In the fight for Empire, as in each man's struggle for life, success means leisure, and therefore civilization, which is the growth of people who have time at their disposal—time to 'create and foster agreeable illusions.' When the Romans conquered the Samnites they were the least artistic people in the world; when Augustus Cæsar died, they possessed and valued the greater part of the world's artistic treasures, many of these already centuries old, and they owned literally, and as slaves, a majority of the best living artists. Augustus had been educated in Athens; he determined that Rome should be as Athens, magnified a hundred times. Athens had her thousand statues, Rome should have her ten thousand; Rome should have state libraries holding a score of volumes for every one that Greece could boast; Rome's temples should be galleries of rare paintings, ten for each that Athens had. Rome should be so great, so rich, so gorgeous, that Greece should be as nothing beside her; Egypt should dwindle to littleness, and the memory of Babylon should be forgotten. Greece had her Homer, her

Sophocles, her Anacreon; Rome should have her immortals also.

Greatly Augustus laboured for his thought, and grandly he carried out his plan. He became the greatest 'art-collector' in all history, and the men of his time imitated him. Domitius Tullus, a Roman gentleman, had collected so much, that he was able to adorn certain extensive gardens, on the very day of the purchase, with an immense number of genuine ancient statues, which had been lying, half neglected, in a barn—or, as some read the passage, in other gardens of his.

BASILICA CONSTANTINE BASILICA CONSTANTINE

Augustus succeeded in one way. Possibly he was successful in his own estimation. 'Have I not acted the play well?' they say he asked, just before he died. The keynote is there, whether he spoke the words or not. He did all from calculation, nothing from conviction. The artist, active and creative or passive and appreciative, calculates nothing except the means of expressing his conviction. And in the over-calculating of effects by Augustus and his successors, one of the most singular weaknesses of the Latin race was thrust forward; namely, that giantism or megalomania, which has so often stamped the principal works of the Latins in all ages—that effort to express greatness by size, which is so conspicuously absent from all that the Greeks have left us. Agrippa builds a threefold temple and Hadrian rears the Pantheon upon its charred ruins; Constantine builds his Basilica; Michelangelo says, 'I will set the Pantheon upon the Basilica of Constantine.' He does it, and the result is Saint Peter's, which covers more ground than that other piece of giantism, the Colosseum; in Rome's last and modern revival, the Palazzo delle Finanze is built, the Treasury of the poorest of the Powers, which, incredible as it may seem, fills a far greater area than either the Colosseum or the Church of Saint Peter's. What else is such constructive enormity but 'giantism'? For the great Cathedral of Christendom, it may be said, at least, that it has more than once in history been nearly filled by devout multitudes, numbering fifty or sixty thousand people; in the days of public baths, nearly sixty-three thousand Romans could bathe daily with every luxury of service; when bread and games were free, a hundred thousand men and women often sat down in the Flavian Amphitheatre to see men tear each other to pieces; of the modern Ministry of Finance there is nothing to be said. The Roman curses it for the millions it cost; but the stranger looks, smiles and passes by a blank and hideous building three hundred yards long. There is no reason why a nation should not wish to be great, but there is every reason why a small nation should not try to look big; and the enormous follies of modern Italy must be charitably attributed to a defect of judgment which has existed in the Latin peoples from the beginning, and has by no means disappeared today. The younger Gordian began a portico which was to cover forty-four thousand square yards, and intended to raise a statue of himself two hundred and nineteen feet high. The modern Treasury building covers about thirty thousand square92 yards, and goes far to rival the foolish Emperor's insane scheme.

RUINS OF THE TEMPLE OF SATURN RUINS OF THE TEMPLE OF SATURN

Great contrasts lie in the past, between his age and ours. One must guess at them at least, if one have but little knowledge, in order to understand at all the city of the Middle Age and the Rome we see today. Imagine it at its greatest, a capital inhabited by more than two millions of souls, filling all that is left to be seen within and without the walls, and half the Campagna besides, spreading out in a vast disc of seething life from the central Golden Milestone at the corner of the temple of Saturn—the god of remote93 ages, and of earth's dim beginning; see, if you can, the splendid roads, where to right and left the ashes of the great rested in tombs gorgeous with marble and gold and bronze; see the endless villas and gardens and terraces lining both banks of the Tiber, with trees and flowers and marble palaces, from Rome to Ostia and the sea, and both banks of the Anio, from Rome to Tivoli in the hills; conceive of the vast commerce, even of the mere business of supply to feed two millions of mouths; picture the great harbour with its thousand vessels—and some of those that brought grain from Egypt were four hundred feet long; remember its vast granaries and store-barns and offices; think of the desolate Isola Sacra as a lovely garden, of the ruins of Laurentum as an imperial palace and park; reckon up roughly what all that meant of life, of power, of incalculable wealth. Mark Antony squandered, in his short lifetime, eight hundred millions of pounds sterling, four thousand millions of dollars. Guess, if possible, at the myriad million details of the vast city.

Then let twelve hundred years pass in a dream, and look at the Rome of Rienzi. Some twenty thousand souls, the remnant and the one hundredth part of the two millions, dwell pitifully in the ruins of which the strongest men have fortified bits here and there. The walls of Aurelian, broken and war-worn and full of half-repaired breaches, enclose a desert, a world too wide for its inhabitants, a vast straggling heterogeneous94 mass of buildings in every stage of preservation and decay, splendid temples, mossy and ivy-grown, but scarcely injured by time, then wastes of broken brick and mortar; stern dark towers of Savelli, and Frangipani, and Orsini, and Colonna, dominating and threatening whole quarters of ruins; strange small churches built of odds and ends and remnants not too heavy for a few workmen to move; broken-down aqueducts sticking up here and there in a city that had to drink the muddy water of the Tiber because not a single channel remained whole to feed a single fountain, from the distant springs that had once filled baths for sixty thousand people every day. And round about all, the waste Campagna, scratched here and there by fever-stricken peasants to yield the little grain that so few men could need. The villas gone, the trees burned or cut down, the terraces slipped away into the rivers, the tombs of the Appian Way broken and falling to pieces, or transformed into rude fortresses held by wild-looking men in rusty armour, who sallied out to fight each other or, at rare intervals, to rob some train of wretched merchants, riding horses as rough and wild as themselves. Law gone, and order gone with it; wealth departed, and self-respect forgotten in abject poverty; each man defending his little with his own hand against the many who coveted it; Rome a den of robbers and thieves; the Pope, when there was one,—there was none in the year of Rienzi's birth,—either defended by95 one baron against another, or forced to fly for his life. Men brawling in the streets, ill clad, savage, ready with sword and knife and club for any imaginable violence. Women safe from none but their own husbands and sons, and not always from them. Children wild and untaught, growing up to be fierce and unlettered like their fathers. And in the midst of such a city, Cola di Rienzi, with great heart and scanty learning, labouring to decipher the inscriptions that told of dead and ruined greatness, dreaming of a republic, of a tribune's power, of the humiliation of the Barons, of a resurrection for Italy and of her sudden return to the dominion of the world.

Rome, then, was like a field long fallow, of rich soil, but long unploughed. Scarcely below the surface lay the treasures of ages, undreamt of by the few descendants of those who had brought them thither. Above ground, overgrown with wild creepers and flowers, there still stood some such monuments of magnificence as we find it hard to recall by mere words, not yet voluntarily destroyed, but already falling to pieces under the slow destruction of grinding time, when violence had spared them. Robert Guiscard had burned the city in , but he had not destroyed everything. The Emperors of the East had plundered Rome long before that, carrying off works of art without end to adorn their city of Constantinople. Builders had burned a thousand marble statues to lime for their cement, for96 the statues were ready to hand and easily broken up to be thrown into the kiln, so that it seemed a waste of time and tools to quarry out the blocks from the temples. The Barbarians of Genseric and the Jews of Trastevere had seized upon such of the four thousand bronze statues as the Emperors had left, and had melted many of them down for metal, often hiding them in strange places while waiting for an opportunity of heating the furnace. And some have been found, here and there, piled up in little vaults, most generally near the Tiber, by which it was always easy to ship the metal away. Already temples had been turned into churches, in a travesty only saved from the ridiculous by the high solemnity of the Christian faith. Other temples and buildings, here and there, had been partly stripped of columns and marble facings to make other churches even more nondescript than the first. Much of the old was still standing, but nothing of the old was whole. The Colosseum had not yet been turned into a quarry. The Septizonium of Septimius Severus, with its seven stories of columns and its lofty terrace, nearly half as high as the dome of Saint Peter's, though beginning to crumble, still crowned the south end of the Palatine; Minerva's temple was almost entire, and its huge architrave had not been taken to make the high altar of Saint Peter's; and the triumphal arch of Marcus Aurelius was standing in what was perhaps not yet called the Corso in those days, but the Via Lata—'Broad Street.'97

The things that had not yet fallen, nor been torn down, were the more sadly grand by contrast with the chaos around them. There was also the difference between ruins then, and ruins now, which there is between a king just dead in his greatness, in whose features lingers the smile of a life so near that it seems ready to come back, and a dried mummy set up in a museum and carefully dusted for critics to study.

In even stronger and rougher contrast, in the wreck of all that had been, there was the fierce reality of the daily fight for life amid the seething elements of the new things that were yet to be; the preparation for another time of domination and splendour; the deadly wrestling of men who meant to outlive one another by sheer strength and grim power of killing; the dark ignorance, darkest just before the waking of new thought, and art, and learning; the universal cruelty of all living things to each other, that had grown out of the black past; and, with all this, the undying belief in Rome's greatness, in Rome's future, in Rome's latent power to rule the world again.

That was the beginning of the new story, for the old one was ended, the race of men who had lived it was gone, and their works were following them, to the universal dust. Out of the memories they left and the departed glory of the places wherein they had dwelt, the magic of the Middle Age was to weave another long98 romance, less grand but more stirring, less glorious but infinitely more human.

Perhaps it is not altogether beyond the bounds of reason to say that Rome was masculine from Romulus to the dark age, and that with the first dawn of the Renascence she began to be feminine. As in old days the Republic and the Empire fought for power and conquest and got both by force, endurance and hardness of character, so, in her second life, others fought for Rome, and courted her, and coveted her, and sometimes oppressed her and treated her cruelly, and sometimes cherished her and adorned her, and gave her all they had. In a way, too, the elder patriots reverenced their city as a father, and those of after-times loved her as a woman, with a tender and romantic love.

Be that as it may, for it matters little how we explain what we feel. And assuredly we all feel that what we call the 'charm,' the feminine charm, of Rome, proceeds first from that misty time between two greatnesses, when her humanity was driven back upon itself, and simple passions, good and evil, suddenly felt and violently expressed, made up the whole life of a people that had ceased to rule by force, and had not yet reached power by diplomacy.

It is fair, moreover, to dwell a little on that time, that we may not judge too hardly the men who came afterwards. If we have any virtues ourselves of which to boast, we owe them to a long growth of civilization, as a child owes its manners to its mother; the men of the Renascence had behind them chaos, the ruin of a slave-ridden, Hun-harried, worm-eaten Empire, in which law and order had gone down together, and the whole world seemed to the few good men who lived in it to be but one degree better than hell itself. Much may be forgiven them, and for what just things they did they should be honoured, for the hardship of having done right at all against such odds.

BRASS OF GORDIAN, SHOWING ROMAN GAMES BRASS OF GORDIAN, SHOWING ROMAN GAMES
RUINS OF THE JULIAN BASILICA RUINS OF THE JULIAN BASILICA

V

Here and there, in out-of-the-way places, overlooked in the modern rage for improvement, little marble tablets are set into the walls of old houses, bearing semi-heraldic devices such as a Crescent, a Column, a Griffin, a Stag, a Wheel and the like. Italian heraldry has always been eccentric, and has shown a tendency to display all sorts of strange things, such as comets, trees, landscapes and buildings in the escutcheon, and it would naturally occur to the stranger that the small marble shields, still visible here and there at the corners of old streets, must be the coats of arms of Roman families that held property in that particular neighbourhood. But this is not the case. They are the distinctive devices of the Fourteen Rioni, or wards, into which the city was divided, with occasional modifications, from the time of Augustus to the coming of Victor Emmanuel, and which with some further changes survive to the present day. The tablets themselves were put up by Pope Benedict the Fourteenth, who reigned from to , and who finally brought them up to the ancient number of fourteen; but from the dark ages the devices themselves were borne upon flags on all public occasions by the people of the different Regions. For 'Rione' is only a corruption of the Latin 'Regio,' the same with our 'Region,' by which English word it will be convenient to speak of these divisions that played so large a part in the history of the city during many successive centuries.

For the sake of clearness, it is as well to enumerate them in their order and with the numbers that have always belonged to each. They are:

I. Monti,
II. Trevi,
III. Colonna,
IV. Campo Marzo,
V. Ponte
VI. Parione,
VII. Regola,
VIII. Sant' Eustachio,
IX. Pigna,
X. Campitelli,
XI. Sant' Angelo,
XII. Ripa,
XIII. Trastevere,
XIV. Borgo.

Five of these names, that is to say, Ponte, Parione, Regola, Pigna and Sant' Angelo, indicate in a general way the part of the city designated by each. Ponte, the Bridge, is the Region about the Bridge of Sant' Angelo, on the left bank at the sharp bend of the river seen from that point; but the original bridge which gave the name was the Pons Triumphalis, of which the foundations are still sometimes visible a little below the Ælian bridge leading to the Mausoleum of Hadrian. Parione, the Sixth ward, is the next division to the preceding one, towards the interior of the city, on both sides of the modern Corso Vittorio Emmanuele, taking in the ancient palace of the Massimo family, the Cancelleria, famous as the most consistent piece of architecture in Rome, and the Piazza Navona. Regola is next, towards the river, comprising the Theatre of Pompey and the Palazzo Farnese. Pigna takes in the Pantheon, the Collegio Romano and the Palazzo di Venezia. Sant' Angelo has nothing to do with the castle or the bridge, but takes its name from the little church of Sant' Angelo in the Fishmarket, and includes the old Ghetto with some neighbouring streets. The rest explain themselves well enough to anyone who has even a very slight acquaintance with the city.

At first sight these more or less arbitrary divisions may seem of little importance. It was, of course, necessary, even in early times, to divide the population and classify it for political and municipal purposes. There is no modern city in the world that is not thus managed by wards and districts, and the consideration of such management and of its means might appear to be a103 very flat and unprofitable study, tiresome alike to the reader and to the writer. And so it would be, if it were not true that the Fourteen Regions of

Rome were fourteen elements of romance, each playing its part in due season, while all were frequently the stage at once, under the collective name of the people, in their ever-latent opposition and in their occasional violent outbreaks against the nobles and the popes, who alternately oppressed and spoiled them for private and public ends. In other words, the Regions with their elected captains under one chief captain were the survival of the Roman People, for ever at odds with the Roman Senate. In times when there was no government, in any reasonable sense of the word, the people tried to govern themselves, or at least to protect themselves as best they could by a rough system which was all that remained of the elaborate municipality of the Empire. Without the Regions the struggles of the Barons would probably have destroyed Rome altogether; nine out of the twenty-four Popes who reigned in the tenth century would not have been murdered and otherwise done to death; Peter the Prefect could not have dragged Pope John the Thirteenth a prisoner through the streets; Stefaneschi could never have terrorized the Barons, and half destroyed their castles in a week; Rienzi could not have made himself dictator; Ludovico Migliorati could not have murdered the eleven captains of Regions in his house and thrown their bodies to the 104 people from the windows, for which Giovanni Colonna drove out the Pope and the cardinals, and sacked the Vatican; in a word, the strangest, wildest, bloodiest scenes of mediæval Rome could not have found a place in history. It is no wonder that to men born and bred in the city the Regions seem even now to be an integral factor in its existence.

There were two other elements of power, namely, the Pope and the Barons. The three are almost perpetually at war, two on a side, against the third. Philippe de Commines, ambassador of Lewis the Eleventh in Rome, said that without the Orsini and the Colonna, the States of the Church would be the happiest country in the world. He forgot the People, and was doubtless too politic to speak of the Popes to his extremely devout sovereign. Take away the three elements of discord, and there would certainly have been peace in Rome, for there would have been no one to disturb the bats and the owls, when everybody was gone.

The excellent advice of Ampère, already quoted, is by no means easy to follow, since there are not many who have the time and the inclination to acquire a 'superficial knowledge' of Rome by a ten years' visit. If, therefore, we merely presuppose an average knowledge of history and a guide-book acquaintance with the chief points in the city, the simplest and most direct way of learning more about it is to take the Regions in their ancient order, as the learned Baracconi has done 105 in his invaluable little work, and to try as far as possible to make past deeds live again where they were done, with such description of the places themselves as may serve the main purpose best. To follow any other plan would be either to attempt a new history of the city of Rome, or to piece together a new archæological manual. In either case, even supposing that one could be successful where so much has already been done by the most learned, the end aimed at would be defeated, for romance would be stiffened to a record, and beauty would be dissected to an anatomical preparation.

BRASS OF TITUS, SHOWING THE COLOSSEUM BRASS OF TITUS, SHOWING THE COLOSSEUM
REGION I MONTI

'Monti' means 'The Hills,' and the device of the Region represents three, figuring those enclosed within the boundaries of this district; namely, the Quirinal, the Esquiline and the Coelian. The line encircling them includes the most hilly part of the mediæval city; beginning at the Porta Salaria, it runs through the new quarter, formerly Villa Ludovisi, to the Piazza Barberini, thence by the Tritone to the Corso, by the Via Marforio, skirting the eastern side of the Capitoline Hill and the eastern side of the Roman Forum to the Colosseum, which it does not include; on almost to the Lateran, back again, so as to include the Basilica, by San Stefano Rotondo, and out by the Navicella to the now closed Porta Metronia. The remainder of the circuit is completed by the Aurelian wall, which is the present107 wall of the city, though the modern Electoral Wards extend in some places beyond it. The modern gates included in this portion are the Porta Salaria, the Porta Pia, the new gate at the end of the Via Montebello, the next, an unnamed opening through which passes the Viale Castro Pretorio, then the Porta Tiburtina, the Porta San Lorenzo, the exit of the railway, Porta Maggiore, and lastly the Porta San Giovanni.

The Region of the Hills takes in by far the largest area of the fourteen districts, but also that portion which in later times has been the least thickly populated, the wildest districts of mediæval and recent Rome, great open spaces now partially covered by new though hardly inhabited buildings, but which were very lately either fallow land or ploughed fields, or cultivated vineyards, out of which huge masses of ruins rose here and there in brown outline against the distant mountains, in the midst of which towered the enormous basilicas of Santa Maria Maggiore and Saint John Lateran, the half-utilized, half-consecrated remains of the Baths of Diocletian, the Baths of Titus, and over against the latter, just beyond the southwestern boundary, the gloomy Colosseum, and on the west the tall square tower of the Capitol with its deep-toned bell, the 'Patarina,' which at last was sounded only when the Pope was dead, and when Carnival was over on Shrove Tuesday night.

It must first be remembered that each Region had108 a small independent existence, with night watchmen of its own, who dared not step beyond the limits of their beat; defined by parishes, there were separate charities for each Region, separate funds for giving dowries to poor girls, separate 'Confraternite' or pious societies to which laymen belonged, and, in a small way, a sort of distinct nationality. There was rivalry between each Region and its neighbours, and when the one encroached upon the other there was strife and bloodshed in the streets. In the public races, of which the last survived in the running of riderless horses through the Corso in Carnival, each Region had its colours, its right of place, and its separate triumph if it won in the contest. There was all that intricate opposition of small parties which arose in every mediæval city, when children followed their fathers' trades from generation to generation, and lived in their fathers' houses from one century to another; and there was all the individuality and the local tradition which never really hindered civilization, but were always an insurmountable barrier against progress.

Some one has called democracy Rome's 'Original Sin.' It would be more just and true to say that most of Rome's misfortunes, and Italy's too, have been the result of the instinct to oppose all that is, whether good or bad, as soon as it has existed for a while; in short, the original sin of Italians is an original detestation of that unity of which the empty name has been109 a fetish for ages. Rome, thrown back upon herself in the dark times, when she was shorn of her possessions, was a true picture of what Italy was before Rome's iron hand had bound the Italian peoples together by force, of what she became again as soon as that force was relaxed, of what she has grown to be once more, now that the delight of revolution has disappeared in the dismal swamp of financial disappointment, of what she will be to all time, because, from all time, she has been populated by races of different descent, who hated each other as only neighbours can.

The redeeming feature of a factional life has sometimes been found in a readiness to unite against foreign oppression; it has often shown itself in an equal willingness to submit to one foreign ruler in order to get rid of another. Circumstances have made the result good or bad. In the year , the Romans attacked and wounded Pope Leo the Third in a solemn procession, almost killed him and drove him to flight, because he had sent the keys of the city to Charles the Great, in self-protection against the splendid, beautiful, gifted, black-hearted Irene, Empress of the East, who had put out her own son's eyes and taken the throne by force. Two years later the people of Rome shouted "Life and Victory to Charles the Emperor," when the same Pope Leo, his scars still fresh, crowned Charlemagne in Saint Peter's. One remembers, for that matter, that Napoleon Bonaparte, crowned in French Paris by another110 Pope, girt on the very sword of that same Frankish Charles, whose bones the

French had scattered to the elements at Aix. Savonarola, of more than doubtful patriotism, to whom Saint Philip Neri prayed, but whom the English historian, Roscoe, flatly calls a traitor, would have taken Florence from the Italian Medici and given it to the French king. Dante was for German Emperors against Italian Popes. Modern Italy has driven out Bourbons and Austrians and given the crown of her Unity to a house of Kings, brave and honourable, but in whose veins there is no drop of Italian blood, any more than their old Dukedom of Savoy was ever Italian in any sense. The glory of history is rarely the glory of any ideal; it is more often the glory of success.

The Roman Republic was the result of internal opposition, and the instinct to oppose power, often rightly, sometimes wrongly, will be the last to survive in the Latin race. In the Middle Age, when Rome had shrunk from the boundaries of civilization to the narrow limits of the Aurelian walls, it produced the hatred between the Barons and the people, and within the people themselves, the less harmful rivalry of the Regions and their Captains.

SANTA FRANCESCA ROMANA SANTA FRANCESCA ROMANA

These Captains held office for three months only. At the expiration of the term, they and the people of their Region proceeded in procession, all bearing olive branches, to the temple of Venus and Rome, of which a part was early converted into the Church of Santa Maria Nuova, now known as Santa Francesca Romana, between the Forum and the Colosseum, and just within the limits of 'Monti.' Down from the hills on the one side the crowd came; up from the regions of the Tiber, round the Capitol from Colonna, and Trevi, and Campo Marzo, as ages before them the people had thronged to the Comitium, only a few hundred yards away. There, before the church in the ruins, each Region dropped the names of its own two candidates into the ballot box, and chance decided which of the two should be Captain next. In procession, then, all round the Capitol, they went to Aracœli, and the single Senator, the lone shadow of the Conscript Fathers, ratified each choice. Lastly, among themselves, they used to choose the Prior, or Chief Captain, until it became the custom that the captain of the First Region, Monti, should of right be head of all the rest, and in reality one of the principal powers in the city.

And the principal church of Monti also held preëminence over others. The Basilica of Saint John Lateran was entitled 'Mother and Head of all Churches of the City and of the World'; and it took its distinctive name from a rich Roman family, whose splendid house stood on the same spot as far back as the early days of the Empire. Even Juvenal speaks of it.

Overthrown by earthquake, erected again at once, twice burned and immediately rebuilt, five times the seat of Councils of the Church, enlarged even in our day at enormous cost, it seems destined to stand on the same spot for ages, and to perpetuate the memory of the Laterans to all time, playing monument to an obscure family of rich citizens, whose name should have been almost lost, but can never be forgotten now.

Constantine, sentimental before he was great, and great before he was a Christian, gave the house of the Roman gentleman to Pope Sylvester. He bought it, or it fell to the crown at the extinction of the family, for he was not the man to confiscate property for a whim; and within the palace he made a church, which was called by more than one name, till after nearly six hundred years it was finally dedicated to Saint John the Baptist; until then it had been generally called the church 'in the Lateran house,' and to this day it is San Giovanni in Laterano. Close by it, in the palace of the Annii, Marcus Aurelius, last of the so-called Antonines, and last of the great emperors, was born and educated; and in his honour was made the famous statue of him on horseback, which now stands in the square of the Capitol. The learned say that it was set up before the house where he was born, and so found itself also before the Lateran in later times, with the older Wolf, at the place of public justice and execution.

In the wild days of the tenth century, when the world was boiling with faction, and trembling at the prospect of the Last Judgment, clearly predicted to overtake mankind in the thousandth year of the Christian era, the whole Roman people, without sanction of the Emperor and without precedent, chose John the Thirteenth to be their Pope. The Regions with their Captains had their way, and the new Pontiff was enthroned114 by their acclamation. Then came their disappointment, then their anger. Pope John, strong, high-handed, a man of order in days of chaos, ruled from the Lateran for one short year, with such wisdom as he possessed, such law as he chanced to have learnt, and all the strength he had. Neither Barons nor people wanted justice, much less learning. The Latin chronicle is brief: 'At that time, Count Roffredo and Peter the Prefect,'—he was the Prior of the Regions' Captains,—'with certain other Romans, seized Pope John, and first threw him into the Castle of Sant' Angelo, but at last drove him into exile in Campania for more than ten months. But when the Count had been murdered by one of the Crescenzi,'—in whose house Rienzi afterwards lived,—'the Pope was released and returned to his See.'

Back came Otto the Great, Saxon Emperor, at Christmas time, as he came more than once, to put down revolution with a strong hand and avenge the wrongs of Pope John by executing all but one of the Captains of the Regions. Twelve of them he hanged. Peter the Prefect, or Prior, was bound naked upon an ass with an earthen jar over his head, flogged through the city, and cruelly put to death; and at last his torn body was hung by the hair to the head of the bronze horse whereon the stately figure of Marcus Aurelius sat in triumph before the door of the Pope's house, as it sits today on the Capitol before the Palace of the Senator. And Otto caused the body of murdered Roffredo to be dragged from its grave and quartered by the hangman and scattered abroad, a warning to the Regions and their leaders. They left Pope John in peace after that, and he lived five years and held a council in the Lateran, and died in his bed. Possibly after his rough experience, his rule was more gentle, and when he was dead he was spoken of as 'that most worthy Pontiff.' Who Count Roffredo was no one can tell surely, but his name belongs to the great house of Caetani.

BASILICA OF ST JOHN LATERAN BASILICA OF ST JOHN LATERAN

It is hard to see past terror in present peace; it is not easy to fancy the rough rabble of Rome in those days, strangely clad, more strangely armed, far out in the waste fields about the Lateran, surging up like demons in the lurid torchlight before the house of the Pope, pressing upon the mailed Count's stout horse, and thronging upon the heels of the Captains and the Prefect, pounding down the heavy doors with stones, and with deep shouts for every heavy blow, while white-robed John and his frightened priests cower together within, expecting death. Down goes the oak with a crash like artillery, that booms along the empty corridors; a moment's pause, and silence, and then the rush, headed by the Knight and the leaders who mean no murder, but mean to have their way, once and for ever, and buffet back their furious followers when they have reached the Pope's116 room, lest he should be torn in pieces. Then, the subsidence of the din, and the old man and his priests bound and dragged out and forced to go on foot by all the long dark way through the city to the black dungeons of Sant' Angelo beyond the rushing river.

SAN GIOVANNI IN LATERANO SAN GIOVANNI IN LATERANO

It seems far away. Yet we who have seen the Roman people rise, overlaid with burdens and maddened by the news of a horrible defeat, can guess at what it must have been. Those who saw the sea of murderous pale faces, and heard the deep cry, 'Death to Crispi,' go howling and echoing through the city can guess what that must have been a thousand years ago, and many another night since then, when the Romans were roused and there was a smell of blood in the air.

But today there is peace in the great Mother of Churches, with an atmosphere of solemn rest that one may not breathe in Saint Peter's nor perhaps anywhere else in Rome within consecrated walls. There is mystery in the enormous pillars that answer back the softest whispered word from niche to niche across the silent aisle; there is simplicity and dignity of peace in the lofty nave, far down and out of jarring distance from the over-gorgeous splendour of the modern transept. In Holy Week, towards evening at the Tenebræ, the divine tenor voice of Padre Giovanni, monk and singer, soft as a summer night, clear as a silver bell, touching as sadness itself, used to float through the dim air with a ring of Heaven in it, full of that strange fatefulness that followed his short life, till he died, nearly twenty years ago, foully poisoned by a layman singer in envy of a gift not matched in the memory of man.

Sometimes, if one wanders upward towards the Monti when the moon is high, a far-off voice rings through the quiet air—one of those voices which hardly ever find their way to the theatre nowadays, and which, perhaps, would not satisfy the nervous taste of our Wagnerian times. Perhaps it sounds better in the moonlight, in those lonely, echoing streets, than it would on the stage. At all events, it is beautiful as118 one hears it, clear, strong, natural, ringing. It belongs to the place and hour, as the humming of honey bees to a field of flowers at noon, or the desolate moaning of the tide to a lonely ocean coast at night. It is not an exaggeration, nor a mere bit of ill nature, to say that there are thousands of fastidiously cultivated people today who would think it all theatrical in the extreme, and would be inclined to despise their own taste if they felt a secret pleasure in the scene and the song. But in Rome even such as they might condescend to the romantic for an hour, because in Rome such deeds have been dared, such loves have been loved, such deaths have been died, that any romance, no matter how wild, has larger probability in the light of what has actually been the lot of real men and women. So going alone through the winding moonlit ways about Tor de' Conti, Santa Maria dei Monti and San Pietro in Vincoli, a man need take no account of modern fashions in sensation; and if he will but let himself be charmed, the enchantment will take hold of him and lead him on through a city of dreams and visions, and memories strange and great, without end. Ever since Rome began there must have been just such silvery nights; just such a voice rang through the same air ages ago; just as now the velvet shadows fell pall-like and unrolled themselves along the grey pavement under the lofty columns of Mars the Avenger and beneath the wall of the Forum of Augustus.

PIAZZA COLONNA PIAZZA COLONNA

Perhaps it is true that the impressions which Rome makes upon a thoughtful man vary more according to the wind and the time of day than those he feels in other cities. Perhaps, too, there is no capital in all the world which has such contrasts to show within a mile of each other—one might almost say within a dozen steps. One of the most crowded thoroughfares of Rome, for instance, is the Via del Tritone, which is the only passage through the valley between the Pincian and the Quirinal hills, from the region of Piazza Colonna towards the railway station and the new quarter. During the busy hours of the day a carriage can rarely move through its 120 narrower portions any faster than at a foot pace, and the insufficient pavements are thronged with pedestrians. In a measure, the Tritone in Rome corresponds to Galata bridge in Constantinople. In the course of the week most of the population of the city must have passed at least once through the crowded little street, which somehow in the rain of millions that lasted for two years, did not manage to attract to itself even the small sum which would have sufficed to widen it by a few yards. It is as though the contents of Rome were daily drawn through a keyhole. In the Tritone are to be seen magnificent equipages, jammed in the line between milk carts, omnibuses and dustmen's barrows, preceded by butcher's vans and followed by miserable cabs, smart dogcarts and high-wheeled country vehicles driven by rough, booted men wearing green-lined cloaks and looking like stage bandits; even saddle horses are led sometimes that way to save time; and on each side flow two streams of human beings of every type to be found between Porta Angelica and Porta San Giovanni. A prince of the Holy Roman Empire pushes past a troop of dirty school children, and is almost driven into an open barrel of salt codfish, in the door of a poor shop, by a black-faced charcoal man carrying a sack on his head more than half as high as himself. A party of jolly young German tourists in loose clothes, with red books in their hands, and their field-glasses hanging by straps across their shoulders, try to rid themselves of 121 the flower-girls dressed in sham Sabine costumes, and utter exclamations of astonishment and admiration when they themselves are almost run down by a couple of the giant Royal Grenadiers, each six feet five or thereabouts, besides nine inches, or so, of crested helmet aloft, gorgeous, gigantic and spotless. Clerks by the dozen and liveried messengers of the ministries struggle in the press; ladies gather their skirts closely, and try to pick a dainty way where, indeed, there is nothing 'dain' (a word which Doctor Johnson confesses that he could not find in any dictionary, but which he thinks might be very useful); servant girls, smart children with nurses and hoops going up to the Pincio, black-browed washerwomen with big baskets of clothes on their heads, stumpy little infantry soldiers in grey uniforms, priests, friars, venders of boot-laces and thread, vegetable sellers pushing hand-carts of green things in and out among the horses and vehicles with amazing dexterity, and yelling their cries in super-humanly high voices—there is no end to the multitude. If the day is showery, it is a sight to see the confusion in the Tritone when umbrellas of every age, material and colour are all opened at once, while the people who have none crowd into the codfish shop and the liquor seller's and the tobacconist's, with traditional 'con permesso' of excuse for entering when they do not mean to buy anything; for the Romans are mostly civil people and fairly good-natured. But rain or shine, at the busy hours, the place is always crowded to overflowing with every description of vehicle and every type of humanity.

Out of Babel—a horizontal Babel—you may turn into the little church, dedicated to the 'Holy Guardian Angel.' It stands on the south side of the Tritone, in that part which is broader, and which a little while ago was still called the Via dell' Angelo Custode—Guardian Angel Street. It is an altogether insignificant little church, and strangers scarcely ever visit it. But going down the Tritone, when your ears are splitting, and your eyes are confused with the kaleidoscopic figures of the scurrying crowd, you may lift the heavy leathern curtain, and leave the hurly-burly outside, and find yourself all alone in the quiet presence of death, the end of all hurly-burly and confusion. It is quite possible that under the high, still light in the round church, with its four niche-like chapels, you may see, draped in black, that thing which no one ever mistakes for anything else; and round about the coffin a dozen tall wax candles may be burning with a steady yellow flame. Possibly, at the sound of the leathern curtain slapping the stone door-posts, as it falls behind you, a sad-looking sacristan may shuffle out of a dark corner to see who has come in; possibly not. He may be asleep, or he may be busy folding vestments in the sacristy. The dead need little protection from the living, nor does a sacristan readily put himself out for nothing. You may stand there undisturbed as long as you please, and see what all the world's noise comes to in the end. Or it may be, if the departed person belonged to a pious confraternity, that you chance upon the brothers of the society—clad in dark hoods with only holes for their eyes, and no man recognized by his neighbour—chanting penitential psalms and hymns for the one whom they all know because he is dead, and they are living.

Such contrasts are not lacking in Rome. There are plenty of them everywhere in the world, perhaps, but they are more striking here, in proportion as the outward forms of religious practice are more ancient, unchanging and impressive. For there is nothing very impressive or unchanging about the daily outside world, especially in Rome.

Rome, the worldly, is the capital of one of the smaller kingdoms of the world, which those who rule it are anxious to force into the position of a great power. One need not criticise their action too hardly; their motives can hardly be anything but patriotic, considering the fearful sacrifices they impose upon their country. But they are not the men who brought about Italian unity. They are the successors of those men; they are not satisfied with that unification, and they have dreamed a dream of ambition, beside which, considering the means at their disposal, the projects of Alexander, Cæsar and Napoleon sink into comparative insignificance. At all events, the worldly, modern, outward124 Italian Rome is very far behind the great European capitals in development, not to say wealth and magnificence. 'Lay' Rome, if one may use the expression, is not in the least a remarkable city. 'Ecclesiastic' Rome is the stronghold of a most tremendous fact, from whatever point of view Christianity may be considered. If one could, in imagination, detach the head of the Catholic Church from the Church, one would be obliged to admit that no single living man possesses the far-reaching and lasting power which in each succeeding papal reign belongs to the Pope. Behind the Pope stands the fact which confers, maintains and extends that power from century to century; a power which is one of the hugest elements of the world's moral activity, both in its own direct action and in the counteraction and antagonism which it calls forth continually.

It is the all-pervading presence of this greatest fact in Christendom which has carried on Rome's importance from the days of the Cæsars, across the chasm of the dark ages, to the days of the modern popes; and its really enormous importance continually throws forward into cruel relief the puerilities and inanities of the daily outward world. It is the consciousness of that importance which makes old Roman society what it is, with its virtues, its vices, its prejudices and its strange, old-fashioned, close-fisted kindliness; which makes the contrast between the Saturnalia of Shrove125 Tuesday night and the cross signed with ashes upon the forehead on Ash Wednesday morning, between the careless laughter of the Roman beauty in Carnival, and the tragic earnestness of the same lovely face when the great lady kneels in Lent, before the confessional, to receive upon her bent head the light touch of the penitentiary's wand, taking her turn, perhaps, with a score of women of the people. It is the knowledge of an always present power, active throughout the whole world, which throws deep, straight shadows, as it were, through the Roman character, just as in certain ancient families there is a secret that makes grave the lives of those who know it.

The Roman Forum and the land between it and the Colosseum, though strictly within the limits of Monti, were in reality a neutral ground, the chosen place for all struggles of rivalry between the Regions. The final destruction of its monuments dates from the sacking of Rome by Robert Guiscard with his Normans and Saracens in the year one thousand and eighty-four, when the great Duke of Apulia came in arms to succour Hildebrand, Pope Gregory the Seventh, against the Emperor Henry the Fourth, smarting under the bitter humiliation of Canossa; and against his Antipope Clement, more than a hundred years after Otto had come back in anger to avenge Pope John. There is no more striking picture of the fearful contest between the Church and the

Empire.

PIAZZA DI SAN GIOVANNI IN LATERANO PIAZZA DI SAN GIOVANNI IN LATERANO

Alexis, Emperor of the East, had sent Henry, Emperor of the Holy Roman Empire, one hundred and forty-four thousand pieces of gold, and one hundred pieces of woven scarlet, as an inducement to make war upon the Norman Duke, the Pope's friend. But the Romans feared Henry and sent ambassadors to him, and on the twenty-first of March, being the Thursday before Palm Sunday, the Lateran gate was opened for him to enter in triumph. The city was divided against itself, the nobles were for Hildebrand, the people were against him. The Emperor seized the Lateran palace and all the bridges. The Pope fled to the Castle of Sant' Angelo, an impregnable fortress in those times, ever ready and ever provisioned for a siege. Of the nobles Henry required fifty hostages as earnest of their neutrality. On the next day he threw his gold to the rabble and they elected his Antipope Gilbert, who called himself Clement the Third, and certain bishops from North Italy consecrated him in the Lateran on Palm Sunday.

Meanwhile Hildebrand secretly sent swift riders to Apulia, calling on Robert Guiscard for help, and still the nobles were faithful to him, and though Henry held the bridges, they were strong in Trastevere and the Borgo, which is the region between the Castle of Sant' Angelo and Saint Peter's. So it turned out that when Henry tried to bring his Antipope in solemn procession to enthrone him in the Pontifical chair, on Easter day, he found mailed knights and footmen waiting for him, and had to fight his way to the Vatican, and forty of his men were killed and wounded in the fray, while the armed nobles lost not one. Yet he reached the Vatican at last, and there he was crowned by the false Pope he had made, with the crown of the Holy Roman Empire. The chronicler apologizes for calling him an emperor at all. Then he set to work to destroy the dwellings of the faithful nobles, and laid siege to the wonderful Septizonium of Severus, in which the true Pope's nephew had fortified himself, and began to batter it down with catapults and battering-rams. Presently came the message of vengeance, brought by one man outriding a host, while the rabble were still128 building a great wall to encircle Sant' Angelo and starve Hildebrand to death or submission, working day and night like madmen, tearing down everything at hand to pile the great stones one upon another. Swiftly came the terrible Norman from the south, with his six thousand horse, Normans and Saracens, and thirty thousand foot, forcing his march and hungry for the Emperor. But Henry fled, making pretext of great affairs in Lombardy, promising great and wonderful gifts to the Roman rabble, and entrusting to their care his imperial city.

Like a destroying whirlwind of fire and steel Robert swept on to the gates and into Rome, burning and slaying as he rode, and sparing neither man, nor woman, nor child, till the red blood ran in rivers between walls of yellow flame. And he took Hildebrand from Sant' Angelo, and brought him back to the Lateran through the reeking ruins of the city in grim and fearful triumph of carnage and destruction.

That was the end of the Roman Forum, and afterwards, when the blood-soaked ashes and heaps of red-hot rubbish had sunk down and hardened to a level surface, the place where the shepherd fathers of Alba Longa had pastured their flocks was called the Campo Vaccino, the Cattle Field, because it was turned into the market for beeves, and rows of trees were planted, and on one side there was a walk where ropes were made, even to our own time.

It became also the fighting ground of the Regions. Among the strangest scenes in the story of the city are those regular encounters between the Regions of Monti and Trastevere which for centuries took place on feast days, by appointment, on the site of the Forum, or occasionally on the wide ground before the Baths of Diocletian. They were battles fought with stones, and far from bloodless. Monti was traditionally of the Imperial or Ghibelline party; Trastevere was Guelph and for the Popes. The enmity was natural and lasting, on a small scale, as it was throughout Italy. The challenge to the fray was regularly sent out by young boys as messengers, and the place and hour were named and the word passed in secret from mouth to mouth. It was even determined by agreement whether the stones were to be thrown by hand or whether the more deadly sling was to be used.

At the appointed time, the combatants appear in the arena, sometimes as many as a hundred on a side, and the tournament begins, as in Homeric times, with taunts and abuse, which presently end in skirmishes between the boys who have come to look on. Scouts are placed at distant points to cry 'Fire' at the approach of the dreaded Bargello and his men, who are the only representatives of order in the city and not, indeed, anxious to face two hundred infuriated slingers for the sake of making peace.

One boy throws a stone and runs away, followed by130 the rest, all prudently retiring to a safe distance. The real combatants wrap their long cloaks about their left arms, as the old Romans used their togas on the same ground, to shield their heads from the blows; a sling whirls half a dozen times like lightning, and a smooth round stone flies like a bullet straight at an enemy's face, followed by a hundred more in a deadly hail, thick and fast. Men fall, blood flows, short deep curses ring through the sunny air, the fighters creep up to one another, dodging behind trees and broken ruins, till they are at cruelly short range; faster and faster fly the stones, and scores are lying prostrate, bleeding, groaning and cursing. Strength, courage, fierce endurance and luck have it at last, as in every battle. Down goes the leader of Trastevere, half dead, with an eye gone, down goes the next man to him, his teeth broken under his torn lips, down half a dozen more, dead or wounded, and the day is lost. Trastevere flies towards the bridge, pursued by Monti with hoots and yells and catcalls, and the thousands who have seen the fight go howling after them, women and children screaming, dogs racing and barking and biting at their heels. And far behind on the deserted Campo Vaccino, as the sun goes down, women weep and frightened children sob beside the young dead. But the next feast day would come, and a counter-victory and vengeance.

That has always been the temper of the Romans; but few know how fiercely it used to show itself in those days. It would have been natural enough that men should meet in sudden anger and kill each other with such weapons as they chanced to have or could pick up, clubs, knives, stones, anything, when fighting was half the life of every grown man. It is harder to understand the murderous stone throwing by agreement and appointment. In principle, indeed, it approached the tournament, and the combat of champions representing two parties is an expression of the ancient instinct of the Latin peoples; so the Horatii and Curiatii fought for Rome and Alba—so Francis the First of France offered to fight the Emperor Charles the Fifth for settlement of all quarrels between the Kingdom and the Empire—and so the modern Frenchman and Italian are accustomed to settle their differences by an appeal to what they still call 'arms,' for the sake of what modern society is pleased to dignify by the name of 'honour.'

But in the stone-throwing combats of Campo Vaccino there was something else. The games of the circus and the bloody shows of the amphitheatre were not forgotten. As will be seen hereafter, bull-fighting was a favourite sport in Rome as it is in Spain today, and the hand-to-hand fights between champions of the Regions were as much more exciting and delightful to the crowd as the blood of men is of more price than the blood of beasts.

The habit of fighting for its own sake, with dangerous weapons, made the Roman rabble terrible when the fray turned quite to earnest; the deadly hail of stones, well aimed by sling and hand, was familiar to every Roman from his childhood, and the sight of naked steel at arm's length inspired no sudden, keen and unaccustomed terror, when men had little but life to lose and set small value on that, throwing it into the balance for a word, rising in arms for a name, doing deeds of blood and flame for a handful of gold or a day of power.

Monti was both the battlefield of the Regions and also, in times early and late, the scene of the most splendid pageants of Church and State. There is a strange passage in the writings of Ammianus Marcellinus, a pagan Roman of Greek birth, contemporary with Pope Damasus in the latter part of the fourth century. Muratori quotes it, as showing what the Bishopric of Rome meant even in those days. It is worth reading, for a heathen's view of things under Valens and Valentinian, before the coming of the Huns and the breaking up of the Roman Empire, and, indeed, before the official disestablishment, as we should say, of the heathen religion; while the High Priest of Jupiter still offered sacrifices on the Capitol, and the six Vestal Virgins still guarded the Seven Holy Things of Rome, and held their vast lands and dwelt in their splendid palace in all freedom of high privilege, as of old.

'For my part,' says Ammianus, 'when I see the magnificence in which the Bishops live in Rome, I am not surprised that those who covet the dignity should use force and cunning to obtain it. For if they succeed, they are sure of becoming enormously rich by the gifts of the devout Roman matrons; they will drive about Rome in their carriages, as they please, gorgeously dressed, and they will not only keep an abundant table, but will give banquets so sumptuous as to outdo those of kings and emperors. They do not see that they could be truly happy if instead of making the greatness of Rome an excuse for their excesses, they would live as some of the Bishops of the Provinces do, who are sparing and frugal, poorly clad and modest, but who make the humility of their manners and the purity of their lives at once acceptable to their God and to their fellow worshippers.'

So much Ammianus says. And Saint Jerome tells how Prætextatus, Prefect of the City, when Pope Damasus tried to convert him, answered with a laugh, 'I will become a Christian if you will make me Bishop of Rome.'

Yet Damasus, famous for the good Latin and beautiful carving of the many inscriptions he composed and set up, was undeniably also a good man in the evil days which foreshadowed the great schism.

SANTA MARIA MAGGIORE SANTA MARIA MAGGIORE

And here, in the year , in the Region of Monti, in the church where now stands Santa Maria Maggiore, a great and terrible name stands out for the first time in history. Orsino, Deacon of the Holy Roman Catholic and Apostolic Church, rouses a party of the people, declares the election of Damasus invalid, proclaims himself Pope in his stead, and officiates as Pontiff in the Basilica of Sicininus. Up from the deep city comes the roaring crowd, furious and hungry for fight; the great doors are closed and Orsino's followers gather round him as he stands on the steps of the altar; but they are few, and those for Damasus are many; down go the doors, burst inward with battering-rams, up135 shoot the flames to the roof, and the short, wild fray lasts while one may count five score, and is over. Orsino and a hundred and thirty-six of his men lie dead on the pavement, the fire licks the rafters, the crowd press outward, and the great roof falls crashing down into wide pools of blood. And after that Damasus reigns eighteen years in peace and splendour. No one knows whether the daring Deacon was of the race that made and unmade popes afterwards, and held half Italy with its fortresses, giving its daughters to kings and taking kings' daughters for its sons, till Vittoria Accoramboni of bad memory began to bring down a name that is yet great. But Orsino he was called, and he had in him much of the lawless strength of those namesakes of his who outfought all other barons but the Colonna, for centuries; and romance may well make him one of them.

Three hundred years later, and a little nearer to us in the dim perspective of the dark ages, another scene is enacted in the same cathedral. Martin the First was afterwards canonized as Saint Martin for the persecutions he suffered at the hands of Constans, who feared and hated him and set up an antipope in his stead, and at last sent him prisoner to die a miserable death in the Crimea. Olympius, Exarch of Italy, was the chosen tool of the Emperor, sent again and again to Rome to destroy the brave Bishop and make way for the impostor. At last, says the greatest136 of Italian chroniclers, fearing the Roman people and their soldiers, he attempted to murder the Pope foully, in hideous sacrilege. To that end he pretended penitence, and begged to be allowed to receive the Eucharist from the Pope himself at solemn high Mass, secretly instructing one of his body-guards to stab the Bishop at the very moment when he should present Olympius with the consecrated bread.

Up to the basilica they went, in grave and splendid procession. One may guess the picture, with its deep colour, with the strong faces of those men, the Eastern guards, the gorgeous robes, the gilded arms, the high sunlight crossing the low nave and falling through the yellow clouds of incense upon the venerable bearded head of the holy man whose death was purposed in the sacred office. First, the measured tread of the Exarch's band moving in order; then, the silence over all the kneeling throng, and upon it the bursting unison of the 'Gloria in Excelsis' from the choir. Chant upon chant as the Pontiff and his Ministers intone the Epistle and the Gospel and are taken up by the singers in chorus at the first words of the Creed. By and by, the Pope's voice alone, still clear and brave in the Preface. 'Therefore with Angels and Archangels, and all the company of Heaven,' he chants, and again the harmony of many voices singing 'Holy, Holy, Holy, Lord God of Sabaoth.' Silence then, at the Consecration, and the dark-browed Exarch bowing to the pavement, beside the paid murderer whose hand is already on his dagger's hilt. 'O Lamb of God, that takest away the sins of the world,' sings the choir in its sad, high chant, and

Saint Martin bows, standing, over the altar, himself communicating, while the Exarch holds his breath, and the slayer fixes his small, keen eyes on the embroidered vestments and guesses how they will look with a red splash upon them.

As the soldier looks, the sunlight falls more brightly on the gold, the incense curls in mystic spiral wreaths, its strong perfume penetrates and dims his senses; little by little, his thoughts wander till they are strangely fixed on something far away, and he no longer sees Pope nor altar nor altar-piece beyond, and is wrapped in a sort of waking sleep that is blindness. Olympius kneels at the steps within the rail, and his heart beats loud as the grand figure of the Bishop bends over him, and the thin old hand with its strong blue veins offers the sacred bread to his open lips. He trembles, and tries to glance sideways to his left with downcast eyes, for the moment has come, and the blow must be struck then or never. Not a breath, not a movement in the church, not the faintest clink of all those gilded arms, as the Saint pronounces the few solemn words, then gravely and slowly turns, with his deacons to right and left of him, and ascends the altar steps once more, unhurt. A miracle, says the chronicler. A miracle, says the amazed soldier, and repeats it upon solemn138 oath. A miracle, says Olympius himself, penitent and converted from error, and ready to save the Pope by all means he has, as he was ready to slay him before. But he only, and the hired assassin beside him, had known what was to be, and the people say that the Exarch and the Pope were already reconciled and agreed against the Emperor.

The vast church has had many names. It seems at one time to have been known as the Basilica of Sicininus, for so Ammianus Marcellinus still speaks of it. But just before that, there is the lovely legend of Pope Liberius' dream. To him and to the Roman patrician, John, came the Blessed Virgin in a dream, one night in high summer, commanding them to build her a church wheresoever they should find snow on the morrow. And together they found it, glistening in the morning sun, and they traced, on the white, the plan of the foundation, and together built the first church, calling it 'Our Lady of Snows,' for Damasus to burn when Orsino seized it,—but the people spoke of it as the Basilica of Liberius. It was called also 'Our Lady of the Manger,' from the relic held holy there; and Sixtus the Third named it 'Our Lady, Mother of God'; and under many popes it was rebuilt and grew, until at last, for its size, it was called, as it is today, 'The Greater Saint Mary's.' At one time, the popes lived near it, and in our own century, when the palace had long been transferred to the Quirinal, a mile to139 northward of the basilica, Papal Bulls were dated 'From Santa Maria Maggiore.'

It is too gorgeous now, too overladen, too rich; and yet it is imposing. The first gold brought from South America gilds the profusely decorated roof, the dark red polished porphyry pillars of the high altar gleam in the warm haze of light, the endless marble columns rise in shining ranks, all is gold, marble and colour.

Many dead lie there, great men and good; and one over whom a sort of mystery hangs, for he was Bartolommeo Sacchi, Cardinal Platina, historian of the Church, a chief member of the famous Roman Academy of the fifteenth century, and a mediæval pagan, accused with Pomponius Letus and others of worshipping false gods; tried, acquitted for lack of evidence; dead in the odour of sanctity; proved at last ten times a heathen, and a bad one, today, by inscriptions found in the remotest part of the Catacombs, where he and his companions met in darkest secret to perform their extravagant rites. He lies beneath the chapel of Sixtus the Fifth, but the stone that marked the spot is gone.

Strange survivals of ideas and customs cling to some places like ghosts, and will not be driven away. The Esquiline was long ago the haunt of witches, who chanted their nightly incantations over the shallow graves where slaves were buried, and under the hideous crosses whereon dead malefactors had groaned away their last hours of life. Mæcenas cleared the land140 and beautified it with gardens, but still the witches came by stealth to their old haunts. The popes built churches and palaces on it, but the dark memories never vanished in the light; and even in our own days, on Saint John's Eve, which is the witches' night of the Latin race, as the Eve of May-day is the Walpurgis of the Northmen, the people went out in thousands, with torches and lights, and laughing tricks of exorcism, to scare away the powers of evil for the year.

On that night the vast open spaces around the Lateran were thronged with men and women and children; against the witches' dreaded influence they carried each an onion, torn up by the roots with stalk and flower; all about, on the outskirts of the place, were kitchen booths, set up with boughs and bits of awnings, yellow with the glare of earthen and iron oil lamps, where snails—great counter-charms against spells—were fried and baked in oil, and sold with bread and wine, and eaten with more or less appetite, according to the strength of men's stomachs. All night, till the early summer dawn, the people came and went, and wandered round and round, and in and out, in parties and by families, to go laughing homeward at last, scarce knowing why they had gone there at all, unless it were because their fathers and mothers had done as they did for generations unnumbered.

BATHS OF DIOCLETIAN BATHS OF DIOCLETIAN

And the Lateran once had another half-heathen festival, on the Saturday after Easter, in memory of the ancient Floralia of the Romans, which had formerly been celebrated on the th of April. It was a most strange festival, now long forgotten, in which Christianity and paganism were blended together. Baracconi, from whom the following account is taken, quotes three sober writers as authority for his description. Yet there is a doubt about the very name of the feast, which is variously called the 'Coromania' and the 'Cornomania.'

On the afternoon of the Saturday in Easter week, say these writers, the priests of the eighteen principal 'deaconries'—an ecclesiastical division of the city long ago abolished and now somewhat obscure—caused the bells to be rung, and the people assembled at their parish churches, where they were received by a 'mansionarius,'—probably meaning here 'a visitor of houses,'—and a layman, who was arrayed in a tunic, and crowned with the flowers of the cornel cherry. In his hand he carried a concave musical instrument of copper, by which hung many little bells. One of these mysterious personages, who evidently represented the pagan element in the ceremony, preceded each parish procession, being followed immediately by the parish priest, wearing the cope. From all parts of the city they went up to the Lateran, and waited before the palace of the Pope till all were assembled.

The Pope descended the steps to receive the homage of the people. Immediately, those of each parish[142] formed themselves into wide circles round their respective 'visitors' and priests, and the strange rite began. In the midst the priest stood still. Round and round him the lay 'visitor' moved in a solemn dance, striking his copper bells rhythmically to his steps, while all the circle followed his gyrations, chanting a barbarous invocation, half Latin and half Greek: 'Hail, divinity of this spot! Receive our prayers in fortunate hour!' and many verses more to the same purpose, and quite beyond being construed grammatically.

The dance is over with the song. One of the parish priests mounts upon an ass, backwards, facing the beast's tail, and a papal chamberlain leads the animal, holding over its head a basin containing twenty pieces of copper money. When they have passed three rows of benches—which benches, by the bye?—the priest leans back, puts his hand behind him into the basin, and pockets the coins.

Then all the priests lay garlands at the feet of the Pope. But the priest of Santa Maria in Via Lata also lets a live fox out of a bag, and the little creature suddenly let loose flies for its life, through the parting crowd, out to the open country, seeking cover. It is like the Hebrew scapegoat. In return each priest receives a golden coin from the Pontiff's hand. The rite being finished, all return to their respective parishes, the dancing 'visitor' still leading the procession. Each143 priest is accompanied then by acolytes who bear holy water, branches of laurel, and baskets of little rolls, or of those big, sweet wafers, rolled into a cylinder and baked, which are called 'cialdoni,' and are eaten to this day by Romans with ice cream. From house to house they go; the priest blesses each dwelling, sprinkling water about with the laurel, and then burning the branch on the hearth and giving some of the rolls to the children. And all the time the dancer slowly dances and chants the strange words made up of some Hebrew, a little Chaldean and a leavening of nonsense.

Jaritan, jaritan, iarariasti
Raphaym, akrhoin, azariasti!

One may leave the interpretation of the jargon to curious scholars. As for the rite itself, were it not attested by trustworthy writers, one would be inclined to treat it as a mere invention, no more to be believed than the legend of Pope Joan, who was supposed to have been stoned to death near San Clemente, on the way to the Lateran.

An extraordinary number of traditions cling to the Region of Monti, and considering that in later times a great part of this quarter was a wilderness, the fact would seem strange. As for the 'Coromania' it seems to have disappeared after the devastation of Monti by Robert Guiscard in , and the general destruction of the city from the Lateran to the Capitol is attributed to144 the Saracens who were with him. But a more logical cause of depopulation is found in the disappearance of water from the upper Region by the breaking of the aqueducts, from which alone it was derived. The consequence of this, in the Middle Age, was that the only obtainable water came from the river, and was naturally taken from it up-stream, towards the Piazza del Popolo, in the neighbourhood of which it was collected in tanks and kept until the mud sank to the bottom and it was approximately fit to drink.

In Imperial times the greater number of the public baths were situated in the Monti. The great Piazza di Termini, now re-named Piazza delle Terme, before the railway station, took its name from the Baths of Diocletian—'Thermæ,' 'Terme,' 'Termini.' The Baths of Titus, the Baths of Constantine, of Philippus, Novatus and others were all in Monti, supplied by the aqueduct of Claudius, the Anio Novus, the Aqua Marcia, Tepula, Julia, Marcia Nova and Anio Vetus. No people in the world were such bathers as the old Romans; yet few cities have ever suffered so much or so long from lack of good water as Rome in the Middle Age. The supply cut off, the whole use of the vast institutions was instantly gone, and the huge halls and porticos and playgrounds fell to ruin and base uses. Owing to their peculiar construction and being purposely made easy of access on all sides, like the temples, the buildings could not even be turned to account by the Barons145 for purposes of fortification, except as quarries for material with which to build their towers and bastions. The inner chambers became hiding-places for thieves, herdsmen in winter penned their flocks in the shelter of the great halls, grooms used the old playground as a track for breaking horses, and round and about the ruins, on feast days, the men of Monti and Trastevere chased one another in their murderous tournaments of stone throwing. A fanatic Sicilian priest saved the great hall of Diocletian's Baths from destruction in Michelangelo's time.

PORTA MAGGIORE, SUPPORTING THE CHANNELS OF THE AQUEDUCT
OF CLAUDIUS AND THE ANIO NOVUS PORTA MAGGIORE, SUPPORTING THE CHANNELS OF THE AQUEDUCT OF CLAUDIUS AND THE ANIO NOVUS

The story is worth telling, for it is little known. In a little church in Palermo, in which the humble146 priest Antonio Del Duca officiated, he discovered under the wall-plaster a beautiful fresco or mosaic of the Seven Archangels, with their names and attributes. Day after day he looked at the fair figures till they took possession of his mind and heart and soul, and inspired him with the apparently hopeless desire to erect a church in Rome in their honour. To Rome he came, persuaded of his righteous mission, to fail of course, after seven years of indefatigable effort. Back to Palermo then, to the contemplation of his beloved angels. And again they seemed to drive him to Rome. Scarcely had he returned when in a dream he seemed to see his ideal church among the ruins of the Baths of Diocletian, which had been built, as tradition said, by thousands of condemned Christians. To dream was to wake with new enthusiasm, to wake was to act. In an hour, in the early dawn, he was in the great hall which is now the Church of Santa Maria degli Angeli, 'Saint Mary of the Angels.'

But it was long before his purpose was finally accomplished. Thirty years of his life he spent in unremitting labour for his purpose, and an accident at last determined his success. He had brought a nephew with him from Sicily, a certain Giacomo Del Duca, a sculptor, who was employed by Michelangelo to carve the great mask over the Porta Pia. Pope Pius the Fourth, for whom the gate was named, praised the stone face to Michelangelo, who told him who had147 made it. The name recalled the sculptor's uncle and his mad project, which appealed to Michelangelo's love of the gigantic. Even the coincidence of appellation pleased the Pope, for he himself had been christened Angelo, and his great architect and sculptor bore an archangel's name. So the work was done in short time, the great church was consecrated, and one of the noblest of Roman buildings was saved from ruin by the poor Sicilian,—and there, in , the heir to the throne of Italy was married with great magnificence, that particular church being chosen because, as a historical monument, it is regarded as the property of the Italian State, and is therefore not under the immediate management of the Vatican. Probably not one in a thousand of the splendid throng that filled the church had heard the name of Antonio Del Duca, who lies buried before the high altar without a line to tell of all he did. So lies Bernini, somewhere in Santa Maria Maggiore, so lies Platina,—he, at least, the better for no epitaph,—and Beatrice Cenci and many others, rest unforgotten in nameless graves.

From the church to the railway station stretch the ruins, continuous, massive, almost useless, yet dear to all who love old Rome. On the south side, there used to be a long row of buildings, ending in a tall old mansion of good architecture, which was the 'Casino' of the great old Villa Negroni. In that house, but recently gone, Thomas Crawford, sculptor, lived for many148 years, and in the long, low studio that stood before what is now the station, but was then a field, he modelled the great statue of Liberty that crowns the Capitol in Washington, and Washington's own monument which stands in Richmond, and many of his other works. My own early childhood was spent there, among the old-time gardens, and avenues of lordly cypresses and of bitter orange trees, and the moss-grown fountains, and long walks fragrant with half-wild roses and sweet flowers that no one thinks of planting now. Beyond, a wild waste of field and broken land led up to Santa Maria Maggiore; and the grand old bells sent their far voices ringing in deep harmony to our windows; and on the Eve of Saint Peter's day, when Saint Peter's was a dream of stars in the distance and the gorgeous fireworks gleamed in the dark sky above the Pincio, we used to climb the high tower above the house and watch the still illumination and the soaring rockets through a grated window, till the last one had burst and spent itself, and we crept down the steep stone steps, half frightened at the sound of our own voices in the ghostly place.

And in that same villa once lived Vittoria Accoramboni, married to Francesco Peretti, nephew of Cardinal Montalto, who built the house, and was afterwards Sixtus the Fifth, and filled Rome with his works in the five years of his stirring reign. Hers also is a story worth telling, for few know it, even among Romans, and it is149 a tale of bloodshed, and of murder, and of all crimes against God and man, and of the fall of the great house of Orsini. But it may better be told in another place, when we reach the Region where they lived and fought and ruled, by terror and the sword.

Near the Baths of Diocletian, and most probably on the site of that same Villa Negroni, too, was that vineyard, or 'villa' as we should say, where Cæsar Borgia and his elder brother, the Duke of Gandia, supped together for the last time with their mother Vanozza, on the night of the th of June, in the year . There has always been a dark mystery about what followed. Many say that Cæsar feared his brother's power and influence with the Pope. Not a few others suggest that the cause of the mutual hatred was a jealousy so horrible to think of that one may hardly find words for it, for its object was their own sister Lucrezia. However that may be, they supped together with their mother in her villa, after the manner of Romans in those times, and long before then, and long since. In the first days of summer heat, when the freshness of spring is gone and June grows sultry, the people of the city have ever loved to breathe a cooler air. In the Region of Monti there were a score of villas, and there were wide vineyards and little groves of trees, such as could grow where there was not much water, or none at all perhaps, saving what was collected in cisterns from the roofs of the few scattered houses, when it rained.

In the long June twilight the three met together, the mother and her two sons, and sat down under an arbour in the garden, for the air was dry with the south wind and there was no fear of fever. Screened lamps and wax torches shed changing tints of gold and yellow on the fine linen, and the deep-chiselled dishes and vessels of silver, and the tall glasses and beakers of many hues. Fruit was piled up in the midst, such as the season afforded, cherries and strawberries, and bright oranges from the south. One may fancy the dark-browed woman of forty years, in the beauty of maturity almost too ripe, with her black eyes and hair of auburn, her jewelled cap, her gold laces just open at her marble throat, her gleaming earrings, her sleeves slashed to show gauze-fine linen, her white, ring-laden fingers that delicately took the finely carved meats in her plate—before forks were used in Rome—and dabbled themselves clean from each touch in the scented water the little page poured over them. On her right, her eldest, Gandia, fair, weak-mouthed, sensually beautiful, splendid in velvet, and chain of gold, and deep-red silk, his blue eyes glancing now and then, half scornfully, half anxiously at his strong brother. And he, Cæsar, the man of infamous memory, sitting there the very incarnation of bodily strength and mental daring; square as a gladiator, dark as a Moor, with deep and fiery eyes, now black, now red in the lamplight, the marvellous smile wreathing his thin lips now and then, and showing151 white, wolfish teeth, his sinewy brown hands direct in every little action, his soft voice the very music of a lie to those who knew the terrible brief tones it had in wrath.

Long they sat, sipping the strong iced wine, toying with fruits and nuts, talking of State affairs, of the Pope, of Maximilian, the jousting Emperor,—discussing, perhaps, with a smile, his love of dress and the beautiful fluted armour which he first invented;—of Lewis the Eleventh of France, tottering to his grave, strangest compound of devotion, avarice and fear that ever filled a throne; of Frederick of Naples, to whom Cæsar was to bear the crown within a few days; of Lucrezia's quarrel with her husband, which had brought her to Rome; and at her name Cæsar's eyes blazed once and looked down at the strawberries on the silver dish, and Gandia turned pale, and felt the chill of the night air, and stately Vanozza rose slowly in the silence, and bade her evil sons good-night, for it was late.

Two hours later, Gandia's thrice-stabbed corpse lay rolling and bobbing at the Tiber's edge, as dead things do in the water, caught by its silks and velvets in wild branches that dipped in the muddy stream; and the waning moon rose as the dawn forelightened.

INTERIOR OF THE COLOSSEUM INTERIOR OF THE COLOSSEUM

If the secrets of old Rome could be known and told, they would fill the world with books. Every stone has tasted blood, every house has had its tragedy, every shrub and tree and blade of grass and wild flower has sucked life from death, and blossoms on a grave. There is no end of memories, in this one Region, as in all the rest. Far up by Porta Pia, over against the new Treasury, under a modern street, lie the bones of guilty Vestals, buried living, each in a little vault two fathoms deep, with the small dish and crust and the earthen lamp that soon flickered out in the close damp air; and there lies that innocent one, Domitian's victim, who shrank from the foul help of the headsman's hand, as her foot slipped on the fatal ladder, and fixed her pure eyes once upon the rabble, and turned and went down alone into the deadly darkness. Down by the Colosseum, where the ruins of Titus' Baths still stand in part, stood Nero's dwelling palace, above the artificial153 lake in which the Colosseum itself was built, and whose waters reflected the flames of the great fire. To northward, in a contrast that leaps ages, rise the huge walls of the Tor de' Conti, greatest of mediæval fortresses built within the city, the stronghold of a dim, great house, long passed away, kinsmen of Innocent the Third. What is left of it helps to enclose a peaceful nunnery.

There were other towers, too, and fortresses, though none so strong as that, when it faced the Colosseum, filled then by the armed thousands of the great Frangipani. The desolate wastes of land in the Monti were ever good battlefields for the nobles and the people. But the stronger and wiser and greater Orsini fortified themselves in the town, in Pompey's theatre, while the Colonna held the midst, and the popes dwelt far aloof on the boundary, with the open country behind them for ready escape, and the changing, factious, fighting city before.

The everlasting struggle, the furious jealousy, the always ready knife, kept the Regions distinct and individual and often at enmity with each other, most of all Monti and Trastevere, hereditary adversaries, Ghibelline and Guelph. Trastevere has something of that proud and violent character still. Monti lost it in the short eruption of 'progress' and 'development.' In the wild rage of speculation which culminated in , its desolate open lands, its ancient villas and its strange154 old houses were the natural prey of a foolish greediness the like of which has never been seen before. Progress ate up romance, and hundreds of acres of wretched, cheaply built, hideous, unsafe buildings sprang up like the unhealthy growth of a foul disease, between the Lateran gate and the old inhabited districts. They are destined to a graceless and ignoble ruin. Ugly cracks in the miserable stucco show where the masonry is already parting, as the hollow foundations subside, and walls on which the paint is still almost fresh are shored up with dusty beams lest they should fall and crush the few paupers who dwell within. Filthy, half-washed clothes of beggars hang down from the windows, drying in the sun as they flap and flutter against pretentious moulded masks of empty plaster. Miserable children loiter in the high-arched gates, under which smart carriages were meant to drive, and gnaw their dirty fingers, or fight for a cold boiled chestnut one of them has saved. Squalor, misery, ruin and vile stucco, with a sprinkling of half-desperate humanity,—those are the elements of the modern picture,—that is what the 'great development' of modern Rome brought forth and left behind it. Peace to the past, and to its ashes of romance and beauty.

REGION II TREVI

In Imperial times, the street now called the Tritone, from the Triton on the fountain in Piazza Barberini, led up from the Portico of Vipsanius Agrippa's sister in the modern Corso to the temple of Flora at the beginning of the Quattro Fontane. It was met at right angles by a long street leading straight from the Forum of Trajan, and which struck it close to the Arch of Claudius. Then, as now, this point was the meeting of two principal thoroughfares, and it was called Trivium, or the 'crossroads.' Trivium turned itself into the Italian 'Trevi,' called in some chronicles 'the Cross of Trevi.' The Arch of Claudius carried the Aqua Virgo, still officially called the Acqua Vergine, across the highway; the water, itself, came to be called the water 'of the crossroads' or 'of Trevi,' and 'Trevi' gave its name at last to the Region, long before the splendid fountain was built in the early part of the last century. The device of the Region seems to have nothing to do with the water, except, perhaps, that the idea of a triplicity is preserved in the three horizontally disposed rapiers.

The legend that tells how the water was discovered gave it the first name it bore. A detachment of Roman soldiers, marching down from Præneste, or Palestrina, in the summer heat, were overcome by thirst, and could find neither stream nor well. A little girl, passing that way, led them aside from the high-road and brought them to a welling spring, clear and icy cold, known only to shepherds and peasants. They drank their fill and called it Aqua Virgo, the Maiden Water. And so it has remained for all ages. But it is commonly called 'Trevi' in Rome, by the people and by strangers, and the name has a ring of poetry, by its associations. For they say that whoever will go to the great fountain, when the high moon rays dance upon the rippling water, and drink, and toss a coin far out into the middle, in offering to the genius of the place, shall surely come back to Rome again, old or young, sooner or later. Many have performed the rite, some secretly, sadly, heartbroken, for love of Rome and what it holds, and others gayly, many together, laughing, while they157 half believe, and sometimes believing altogether while they laugh. And some who loved, and could meet only in Rome, have gone there together, and women's tears have sometimes dropped upon the silvered water that reflected the sad faces of grave men.

The foremost memories of the past in Trevi centre about the ancient family of the Colonna, still numerous, distinguished and flourishing after a career of nearly a thousand years—longer than that, it may be, if one take into account the traditions of them that go back beyond the earliest authentic mention of their greatness; a race of singular independence and energy, which has given popes to Rome, and great patriots, and great generals as well, and neither least nor last, Vittoria, princess and poetess, whose name calls up the gentlest memories of Michelangelo's elder years.

The Colonna were originally hill men. The earliest record of them tells that their great lands towards Palestrina were confiscated by the Church, in the eleventh century. The oldest of their titles is that of Duke of Paliano, a town still belonging to them, rising on an eminence out of the plain beyond the Alban hills. The greatest of their early fortresses was Palestrina, still the seat and title estate of the Barberini branch of the family. Their original stronghold in Rome was almost on the site of their present palace, being then situated on the opposite side of the Basilica of the Santi Apostoli, where the headquarters of the158 Dominicans now are, and running upwards and backwards, thence, to the Piazza della Pilotta; but they held Rome by a chain of towers and fortifications, from the Quirinal to the Mausoleum of Augustus, now hidden among the later buildings, between the Corso, the Tiber, the Via de' Pontefici and the Via de' Schiavoni. The present palace and the basilica stood partly upon the site of the ancient quarters occupied by the first Cohort of the Vigiles, or city police, of whom about seven thousand preserved order when the population of ancient Rome exceeded two millions.

The 'column,' from which the Colonna take their name, is generally supposed to have stood in the market-place of the village of that name in the higher part of the Campagna, between the Alban and the Samnite hills, on the way to Palestrina. It is a peaceful and vine-clad country, now. South of it rise the low heights of Tusculum, and it is more than probable that the Colonna were originally descended from the great counts who tyrannized over Rome from that strong point of vantage and, through them, from Theodora Senatrix. Be that as it may, their arms consist of a simple column, used on a shield, or as a crest, or as the badge of the family, and it is found in many a threadbare tapestry, in many a painting, in the frescos and carved ornaments of many a dim old church in Rome.

FOUNTAIN OF TREVI FOUNTAIN OF TREVI

In their history, the first fact that stands out is their adherence to the Emperors, as Ghibellines, whereas their rivals, the Orsini, were Guelphs and supporters of the Church in most of the great contests of the Middle Age. The exceptions to the rule are found when the Colonna had a Pope of their own, or one who, like Nicholas the Fourth, was of their own making. 'That Pope,' says Muratori, 'had so boundlessly favoured the aggrandizement of the Colonna that his actions depended entirely upon their dictates, and a libel was published upon him, entitled the Source of Evil, illustrated by a caricature, in which the mitred head of the Pontiff was seen issuing from a tall column between two smaller ones, the latter intended to represent the two living cardinals of the house, Jacopo and Pietro.' Yet in the next reign, when they impeached the election of Boniface the Eighth, they found themselves in opposition to the Holy See, and they and theirs were almost utterly destroyed by the Pope's partisans and kinsmen, the powerful Caetani.

Just before him, after the Holy See had been vacant for two years and nearly four months, because the Conclave of Perugia could not agree upon a Pope, a humble southern hermit of the Abruzzi, Pietro da Morrone, had been suddenly elevated to the Pontificate, to his own inexpressible surprise and confusion, and after a few months of honest, but utterly fruitless, effort to understand and do what was required of him, he had taken the wholly unprecedented step of abdicating the160 papacy. He was succeeded by Benedict Caetani, Boniface the Eighth, keen, learned, brave, unforgiving and the mortal foe of the Colonna; 'the magnanimous sinner,' as Gibbon quotes from a chronicle, 'who entered like a fox, reigned like a lion and died like a dog.' Yet the judgment is harsh, for though his sins were great, the expiation was fearful, and he was brave as few men have been.

Samson slew a lion with his hands, and the Philistines with the jaw-bone of an ass. Men have always accepted the Bible's account of the slaughter. But when an ass, without the aid of any Samson, killed a lion in the courtyard of the

Palazzo dei Priori, in Florence, the event was looked upon as of evil portent, exceeding the laws of nature. For Pope Boniface had presented the Commonwealth of Florence with a young and handsome lion, which was chained up and kept in the court of the palace aforesaid. A donkey laden with firewood was driven in, and 'either from fear, or by a miracle,' as the chronicle says, at once assailed the lion with the utmost ferocity, and kicked him to death, in spite of the efforts of a number of men to drag the beast of burden off. Of the two hypotheses, the wise men of the day preferred the supernatural explanation, and one of them found an ancient Sibylline prophecy to the effect that 'when the tame beast should kill the king of beasts, the dissolution of the Church should begin.' Which saying, adds Villani, was presently fulfilled in Pope Boniface.

For the Pope had a mortal quarrel with Philip the Fair of France whom he had promised to make Emperor, and had then passed over in favour of Albert, son of Rudolph of Hapsburg; and Philip made a friend and ally of Stephen Colonna, the head of the great house, who was then in France, and drove Boniface's legate out of his kingdom, and allowed the Count of Artois to burn the papal letters. The Pope retorted by a Major Excommunication, and the quarrel became furious. The Colonna being under his hand, Boniface vented his anger upon them, drove them from Rome, destroyed their houses, levelled Palestrina to the ground, and ploughed up the land where it had stood. The six brothers of the house were exiles and wanderers. Old Stephen, the idol of Petrarch, alone and wretched, was surrounded by highwaymen, who asked who he was. 'Stephen Colonna,' he answered, 'a Roman citizen.' And the thieves fell back at the sound of the great name. Again, someone asked him with a sneer where all his strongholds were, since Palestrina was gone. 'Here,' he answered, unmoved, and laying his hand upon his heart. Of such stuff were the Pope's enemies.

Nor could he crush them. Boniface was of Anagni, a city of prehistoric walls and ancient memories which belonged to the Caetani; and there, in the late summer, he was sojourning for rest and country air, with his cardinals and his court and his kinsmen about him. Among the cardinals was Napoleon Orsini.

GRAND HALL OF THE COLONNA PALACE GRAND HALL OF THE COLONNA PALACE

Then came William of Nogaret, sent by the King of France, and Sciarra Colonna, the boldest man of his day, and many other nobles, with three hundred knights and many footmen. For a long time they had secretly plotted a master-stroke of violence, spending money freely among the people, and using all persuasion to bring the country to their side, yet with such skill and caution that not the slightest warning reached the Pope's ears. In calm security he rose early on the morning of the seventh of September. He believed his position assured, his friends loyal and the Colonna ruined for ever; and Colonna was at the gate.

Suddenly, from below the walls, a cry of words came up to the palace windows; long drawn out, distinct in the still mountain air. 'Long live the King of France! Death to Pope Boniface!' It was taken up by hundreds of voices, and repeated, loud, long and terrible, by the people of the town, by men going out to their work in the hills, by women loitering on their doorsteps, by children peering out, half frightened, from behind their mothers' scarlet woollen skirts, to see the armed men ride up the stony way. Cardinals, chamberlains, secretaries, men-at-arms, fled like sheep; and when Colonna reached the palace wall, only the Pope's own kinsmen remained within to help him as they could, barring the great doors and posting themselves with crossbows at the grated window. For the Caetani were always brave men.

But Boniface knew that he was lost, and calmly, courageously, even grandly, he prepared to face death. 'Since I am betrayed,' he said, 'and am to die, I will at least die as a Pope should!' So he put on the great pontifical chasuble, and set the tiara of Constantine upon his head, and, taking the keys and the crosier in his hands, sat down on the papal throne to await death.

The palace gates were broken down, and then there was no more resistance, for the defenders were few. In a moment Colonna in his armour stood before the Pontiff in his robes; but he saw only the enemy of his race, who had driven out his great kinsmen, beggars and wanderers on the earth, and he lifted his visor and looked long at his victim, and then at last found words for his wrath, and bitter reproaches and taunts without end and savage curses in the broad-spoken Roman tongue. And William of Nogaret began to speak, too, and threatened to take Boniface to Lyons where a council of the Church should depose him and condemn him to ignominy. Boniface answered that he should expect nothing better than to be deposed and condemned by a man whose father and mother had been publicly burned for their crimes. And this was true of Nogaret, who was no gentleman. A legend says that Colonna struck the Pope in the face, and that he afterwards made him ride on an ass, sitting backwards, after the manner of the times. But no trustworthy chronicle tells of this. On the contrary, no one laid hands upon him while he was kept a prisoner under strict watch for three days, refusing to touch food; for even if he could have eaten he feared poison. And Colonna tried to force him to abdicate, as Pope Celestin had done before him, but he refused stoutly; and when the three days were over, Colonna went away, driven out, some say, by the people of Anagni who turned against him. But that is absurd, for Anagni is a little place and Colonna had a strong force of good soldiers with him. Possibly, seeing that the old man refused to eat, Sciarra feared lest he should be said to have starved the Pope to death. They went away and left him, carrying off his treasures with them, and he returned to Rome, half mad with anger, and fell into the hands of the Orsini cardinals, who judged him not sane and kept him a prisoner at the Vatican, where he died soon afterwards, consumed by his wrath. And before long the Colonna had their own again and rebuilt Palestrina and their palace in Rome.

Twenty-five years later they were divided against each other, in the wild days when Lewis the Bavarian, excommunicated and at war with the Pope, was crowned and consecrated Emperor, by the efforts of an extraordinary man of genius, Castruccio degli Interminelli, known better as Castruccio Castracane, the Ghibelline lord of Lucca who made Italy ring with his deeds for twenty years, and died of a fever, in the height of his success and glory, at the age of forty-seven years. Sciarra Colonna was for him and for Lewis. Stephen, head of the house, was against them, and in those days when Rome was frantic for an Emperor, Stephen's son Jacopo had the quiet courage to bring out the Bull of Excommunication against the chosen Emperor and nail it to the door of San Marcello, in the Corso, in the heart of Rome and in the 166 sight of a thousand angry men, in protest against what they meant to do—against what was doing even at that moment. And he reached Palestrina in safety, shaking the dust of Rome from his feet.

But on that bright winter's day, Lewis of Bavaria and his queen rode down from Santa Maria Maggiore by the long and winding ways towards Saint Peter's. The streets were all swept and strewn with yellow sand and box leaves and myrtle that made the air fragrant, and from every window and balcony gorgeous silks and tapestries were hung, and even ornaments of gold and silver and jewels. Before the procession rode standard-bearers, four for each Region, on horses most richly caparisoned. There rode Sciarra Colonna, and beside him, for once in history, Orsino Orsini, and others, all dressed in cloth of gold, and Castruccio Castracane, wearing that famous sword which in our own times was offered by Italy to King Victor Emmanuel; and many other Barons rode there in splendid array, and there was great concourse of the people. So they came to Saint Peter's; and because the Count of the Lateran should by right have been the Emperor's sponsor at the anointing, and had left Rome in anger and disdain, Lewis made Castruccio a knight of the Empire and Count of the Lateran in his stead, and sponsor; and two excommunicated Bishops consecrated the Emperor, and anointed him, and Sciarra Colonna crowned him and his queen. After which they feasted in the evening 167 at the Aracœli, and slept in the Capitol, because they were all weary with the long ceremony, and it was too late to go home. The chronicler's comment is curious. 'Note,' he says, 'what presumption was this, of the aforesaid damned Bavarian, such as thou shalt not find in any ancient or recent history; for never did any Christian Emperor cause himself to be crowned save by the Pope or his legate, even though opposed to the Church, neither before then nor since, except this Bavarian.' But Sciarra and Castruccio had their way, and Lewis did what even Napoleon, master of the world by violent chance, would not do. And twenty years later, in the same chronicle, it is told how 'Lewis of Bavaria, who called himself Emperor, fell with his horse, and was killed suddenly, without penitence, excommunicated and damned by Holy Church.' It is a curious coincidence that Boniface the Eighth, Sciarra's prisoner, and Lewis the Bavarian, whom he crowned Emperor, both died on the eleventh of October, according to most authorities.

The Senate of Rome had dwindled to a pitiable office, held by one man. At or about this time, the Colonna and the Orsini agreed by a compromise that there should be two, chosen from their two houses. The Popes were in Avignon, and men who could make Emperors were more than able to do as they pleased with a town of twenty or thirty thousand inhabitants, so long as the latter had no leader. One may judge of 168 what Rome was, when even pilgrims did not dare to go thither and visit the tomb of Saint Peter. The discord of the great houses made Rienzi's life a career; the defection of the Orsini from the Pope's party led to his flight; their battles suggested to the exiled Pope the idea of sending him back to Rome to break their power and restore a republic by which the Pope might restore himself; and the rage of their retainers expended itself in his violent death. For it was their retainers who fought for their masters, till the younger Stephen Colonna killed Bertoldo Orsini, the bravest man of his day, in an ambush, and the Orsini basely murdered a boy of the Colonna on the steps of a church. But Rienzi was of another Region, of the Regola by the Tiber, and it is not yet time to tell his story. And by and by, as the power of the Popes rose and they became again as the Cæsars had been, Colonna and Orsini forgot their feuds, and were glad to stand on the Pope's right and left as hereditary 'Assistants of the Holy See.' In the petty ending of all old greatnesses in modern times, the result of the greatest feud that ever made two races mortal foes is merely that no prudent host dare ask the heads of the two houses to dinner together, lest a question of precedence should arise, such as no master of ceremonies would presume to settle. That is what it has come to. Once upon a time an Orsini quarrelled with a Colonna in the Corso, just where Aragno's café is now 169 situated, and ran him through with his rapier, wounding him almost to death. He was carried into the palace of the Theodoli, close by, and the records of that family tell that within the hour eight hundred of the Colonna's retainers were in the house to guard him. In as short space, the Orsini called out three thousand men in arms, when Cæsar Borgia's henchman claimed the payment of a tax.

INTERIOR OF THE MAUSOLEUM OF AUGUSTUS INTERIOR OF THE MAUSOLEUM OF AUGUSTUS

From a print of the last century

Times have changed since then. The Mausoleum of Augustus, once a fortress, has been an open air theatre in our time, and there the great Salvini and Ristori often acted in their early youth; it is a circus now. And in less violent contrast, but with change as great from what it was, the palace of the Colonna suggests no thought of defence nowadays, and the wide gates and courtyard recall rather the splendours of the Constable and of his wife, Maria Mancini, niece of Cardinal Mazarin, than the fiercer days when Castracane was Sciarra's guest on the other side of the church.

The Basilica of the Apostles is said to have been built by Pelagius the First, who was made Pope in the year , and who dedicated it to Saint Philip and Saint James. Recent advances in the study of archæology make it seem more than probable that he adapted for the purpose a part of the ancient barracks of the Vigiles, of which the central portion appears almost to coincide with the present church, at a somewhat different angle; and in the same way it is likely that the remains of the north wing were rebuilt at a later period by the Colonna as a fortified palace. In those times men would not have neglected to utilize the massive substructures and walls. However that may be, the Colonna dwelt there at a very early date, and in eight hundred years or more have only removed their headquarters from one side of the church to the other. The latter has been changed and rebuilt, and altered again, like most of the great Roman sanctuaries, till it bears no resemblance to the original building. The present church is distinctly ugly, with the worst defects of the early eighteenth century; and that age was as deficient in cultivated taste as it was abhorrent of natural beauty. Some fragments of the original frescos that adorned the apse are now preserved in a hall behind the main Sacristy of Saint Peter's. Against the flat walls, under the inquisition of the crudest daylight, the fragments of Melozzo da Forli's masterpiece are masterpieces still; the angelic faces, imprisoned in a place not theirs, reflect the sadness of art's captivity; and the irretrievable destruction of an inimitable past excites the pity and resentment of thoughtful men. The attempt to outdo the works of the great has exhibited the contemptible imbecility of the little, and the coarse-grained vanity of Clement the Eleventh has parodied the poetry of art in the bombastic prose of a vulgar tongue. Pope Pelagius took for his church the pillars and marbles of Trajan's Forum, in the belief that his acts were acceptable to God; but Clement had no such excuse, and the edifice which was a monument of faith has given place to the temple of a monumental vanity.

FORUM OF TRAJAN FORUM OF TRAJAN

It is remarkable that the Colonna rarely laid their dead in the Church of the Apostles, for it was virtually theirs by right of immediate neighbourhood, and during their domination they could easily have assumed actual possession of it as a private property. A very curious custom, which survived in the sixteenth century, and perhaps much later, bears witness to the close connection between their family and the church. At that time a gallery existed, accessible from the palace and looking down into the basilica, so that the family could assist at Mass without leaving their dwelling.

On the afternoon of the first of May, which is the traditional feast of this church, the poor of the neighbourhood assembled within. The windows of the palace gallery were then thrown open and a great number of fat fowls were thrown alive to the crowd, turkeys, geese and the like, to flutter down to the pavement and be caught by the luckiest of the people in a tumultuous scramble. When this was over, a young pig was swung out and lowered in slings by a purchase of which the block was seized to a roof beam. When just out of reach the rope was made173 fast, and the most active of the men jumped for the animal from below, till one was fortunate enough to catch it with his hands, when the rope was let go, and he carried off the prize. The custom was evidently similar to that of climbing the May-pole, which was set up on the same day in the Campo Vaccino. May-day was one of the oldest festivals of the Romans, for it was sacred to the tutelary Lares, or spirits of ancestors, and was kept holy, both publicly by the whole city as the habitation of the Roman people, and by each family in its private dwelling. It is of Aryan origin and is remembered in one way or another by all Aryan races in our own time, and it is not surprising that in the general conversion of Paganism to Christianity a new feast should have been intentionally made to coincide with an old one; but it is hard to understand the lack of all reverence for sacred places which could admit such a scene as the scrambling for live fowls and pigs in honour of the twelve Apostles, a pious exercise which is perhaps paralleled, though assuredly not equalled, in crudeness, by the old Highland custom of smoking tobacco in kirk throughout the sermon.

At the very time when we have historical record of a Pope's presence as an amused spectator of the proceedings, Michelangelo had lately painted the ceiling of the Sixtine chapel, and had not yet begun his Last Judgment; and 'Diva' Vittoria Colonna, not174 yet the friend of his later years, was perhaps even then composing those strangely passionate spiritual sonnets which appeal to the soul through the heart, by the womanly pride that strove to make the heart subject to the soul.

The commonplace romance which has represented Vittoria Colonna and Michelangelo as in love with each other is as unworthy of both as it is wholly without foundation. They first met nine years before her death, when she was almost fifty and he was already sixty-four. She had then been widowed twelve years, and it was long since she had refused in Naples the princely suitors who made overtures for her hand. The true romance of her life was simpler, nobler and more enduring, for it began when she was a child, and it ended when she breathed her last in the house of Giuliano Cesarini, the kinsman of her people, whose descendant married her namesake in our own time.

At the age of four, Vittoria was formally betrothed to Francesco d'Avalos, heir of Pescara, one of that fated race whose family history has furnished matter for more than one stirring tale. Vittoria was born in Marino, the Roman town and duchy which still gives its title to Prince Colonna's eldest son, and she was brought up in Rome and Naples, of which latter city her father was Grand Constable. Long before she was married, she saw her future husband and175 loved him at first sight, as she loved him to her dying day, so that although even greater offers were made for her, she steadfastly refused to marry any other man. They were united when she was seventeen years old, he loved her devotedly, and they spent many months together almost without other society in the island of Ischia. The Emperor Charles the Fifth was fighting his lifelong fight with Francis the First of France. Colonna and Pescara were for the Empire, and Francesco d'Avalos joined the imperial army; he was taken prisoner at Ravenna and carried captive to France; released, he again fought for Charles, who offered him the crown of the kingdom of Naples; but he refused it, and still he fought on, to fall at last at Pavia, in the strength of his mature manhood, and to die of his wounds in Milan when Vittoria was barely five and thirty years of age, still young, surpassingly beautiful, and gifted as few women have ever been. What their love was, their long correspondence tells,—a love passionate as youth and enduring as age, mutual, whole and faithful. For many years the heartbroken woman lived in Naples, where she had been most happy, feeding her soul with fire and tears. At last she returned to Rome, to her own people, in her forty-ninth year. There she was visited by the old Emperor for whom her husband had given his life, and there she met Michelangelo.

It was natural enough that they should be friends. It is monstrous to suppose them lovers. The melancholy of their natures drew them together, and the sympathy of their tastes cemented the bond. To the woman-hating man of genius, this woman was a revelation and a wonder; to the great princess in her perpetual sorrow the greatest of creative minds was a solace and a constant intellectual delight. Their friendship was mutual, fitting and beautiful, which last is more than can be said for the absurd stories about their intercourse which are extant in print and have been made the subject of imaginary pictures by more than one painter. The tradition that they used to meet often in the little Church of Saint Sylvester, behind the Colonna gardens, rests upon the fact that they once held a consultation there in the presence of Francesco d'Olanda, a Portuguese artist, when Vittoria was planning the Convent of Saint Catherine, which she afterwards built not very far away. The truth is that she did not live in the palace of her kinsfolk after her return to Rome, but most probably in the convent attached to the other and greater Church of Saint Sylvester which stands in the square of that name not far from the Corso. The convent itself is said to have been originally built for the ladies of the Colonna who took the veil, and was only recently destroyed to make room for the modern Post-office, the church itself having passed into the hands of the English. The coincidence of the two churches being dedicated to the same saint doubtless[177] helped the growth of the unjust fable. But in an age of great women, in the times of Lucrezia Borgia, great and bad, of Catherine Sforza, great and warlike, Vittoria Colonna was great and good; and the ascetic Michelangelo, discovering in her the realization of an ideal, laid at her feet the homage of a sexagenarian's friendship.

In the battle of the archæologists the opposing forces traverse and break ground, and rush upon each other again, 'hurtling together like wild boars,'—as Mallory describes the duels of his knights,—and when learned doctors disagree it is not the province of a searcher after romance to attempt a definition of exact truths. 'Some romances entertain the genius,' quotes Johnson, 'and strengthen it by the noble ideas which they give of things; but they corrupt the truth of history.'

Professor Lanciani, who is probably the greatest authority, living or dead, on Roman antiquities, places the site of the temple of the Sun in the Colonna gardens, and another writer compares the latter to the hanging gardens of Babylon, supported entirely on ancient arches and substructures rising high above the natural soil below. But before Aurelian erected the splendid building to record his conquest of Palmyra, the same spot was the site of the 'Little Senate,' instituted by Elagabalus in mirthful humour, between an attack of sacrilegious folly and a fit of cruelty.

The 'Little Senate' was a woman's senate; in other[178] words, it was a regular assembly of the fashionable Roman matrons of the day, who met there in hours of idleness under the presidency of the Emperor's mother, Semiamira. Ælius Lampridius, quoted by Baracconi, has a passage about it. 'From this Senate,' he says, 'issued the absurd laws for the matrons, entitled Semiamiran Senatorial Decrees, which determined for each matron how she might dress, to whom she must yield precedence, by whom she might be kissed, deciding which ladies might drive in chariots, and which in carts, and whether the latter should be drawn by caparisoned horses, or by asses, or by mules, or oxen; who should be allowed to be carried in a litter or a chair, which might be of leather or of bone with fittings of ivory or of silver, as the case might be; and it was even determined which ladies might wear shoes adorned only with gold, and which might have gems set in their boots.' Considering how little human nature has changed in eighteen hundred years it is easy enough to imagine what the debates in the 'Little Senate' must have been with Semiamira in the chair ruling everything 'out of order' which did not please her capricious fancy: the shrill discussions about a fashionable head-dress, the whispered intrigues for a jewel-studded slipper, the stormy divisions on the question of gold hairpins, and the atmosphere of beauty, perfumes, gossip, vanity and all feminine dissension. But the 'Little Senate' was short-lived.

Some fifty years after Elagabalus, Aurelian triumphed over Zenobia of Palmyra, and built his temple of the Sun. That triumph was the finest sight, perhaps, ever seen in imperial Rome. Twenty richly caparisoned elephants and two hundred captive wild beasts led the immense procession; eight hundred pairs of gladiators came next, the glory and strength of fighting manhood, with all their gleaming arms and accoutrements, marching by the huge Flavian Amphitheatre, where sooner or later they must fight each other to the death; then countless captives of the East and South and West and North, Syrian nobles, Gothic warriors, Persian dignitaries beside Frankish chieftains, and Tetricus, the great Gallic usurper, in the attire of his nation, with his young son whom he had dared to make a Senator in defiance of the Empire. Three royal equipages followed, rich with silver, gold and precious stones, one of them Zenobia's own, and she herself seated therein, young, beautiful, proud and vanquished, loaded from head to foot with gems, most bitterly against her will, her hands and feet bound with a golden chain, and about her neck another, long and heavy, of which the end was held by a Persian captive who walked beside the chariot and seemed to lead her. Then Aurelian, the untiring conqueror, in the car of the Gothic king, drawn by four great stags, which he himself was to sacrifice to Jove that day according to his vow, and a long line of wagons loaded down and groaning under180 the weight of the vast spoil; the Roman army, horse and foot, the Senate and the people, a million, perhaps, all following the indescribable magnificence of the great triumph, along the Sacred Way, that was yellow with fresh strewn sand and sweet with box and myrtle.

RUINS OF HADRIAN'S VILLA AT TIVOLI RUINS OF HADRIAN'S VILLA AT TIVOLI

But when it was over, Aurelian, who was generous when he was not violent, honoured Zenobia and endowed her with great fortune, and she lived for many years as a Roman Matron in Hadrian's villa at Tivoli. And the Emperor made light of the 'Little Senate' and built his Sun temple on the spot, with singular magnificence, enriching its decoration with pearls and precious stones and with fifteen thousand pounds in weight of pure gold. Much of that temple was still standing in181 the seventeenth century and was destroyed by Urban the Eighth, the Pope who built the heavy round tower on the south side of the Quirinal palace, facing Monte Cavallo.

Monte Cavallo itself was a part of the Colonna villa, and its name, only recently changed to Piazza del Quirinale, was given to it by the great horses that stand on each side of the fountain, and which were found long ago, according to tradition, between the Palazzo Rospigliosi and the Palazzo della Consulta. In the times of Sixtus the Fifth, they were in a pitiable state, their forelegs and tails gone, their necks broken, their heads propped up by bits of masonry. When he finished the Quirinal palace he restored them and set them up, side by side, before the entrance, and when Pius the Sixth changed their position and turned them round, the ever conservative and ever discontented Roman people were disgusted by the change. On the pedestal of one of them are the words, 'Opus Phidiae,' 'the work of Phidias,' A punning placard was at once stuck upon the inscription with the legend, 'Opus Perfidiae Pii Sexti'—'the work of perfidy of Pius the Sixth.'

The Quirinal palace cannot be said to have played a part in the history of Rome. Its existence is largely due to the common sense of Sixtus the Fifth, and to his love of good air. He was a shepherd by birth, and it is recorded that the first of his bitter disappointments182 was that the farmer whom he served set him to feed the pigs because he could not learn how to drive sheep to pasture; a disgrace which ultimately made him run away, when he fell in with a monk whose face he liked. He informed the astonished father that he meant to follow him everywhere, 'to Hell, if he chose,'—which was a forcible if not a pious resolution,—and explained that the pigs would find their way home alone. Later, when he had quarrelled with all the monks in Naples, including his superiors, he came to Rome, and, being by that time very learned, he was employed to expound the 'Formalities' of Scotus to the 'Signor' Marcantonio Colonna, abbot of the Monastery of the Apostles; and there he resided as a guest for a long time till his brilliant pupil was himself master of the subject, as well as a firm friend of the quarrelsome monk; and in their intercourse the seeds were no doubt sown of that implacable hatred against the Orsini which, under the great and just provocation of a kinsman's murder, ended in the exile and temporary ruin of the Colonna's rivals. No doubt, also, the abbot and the monk often strolled together in the Colonna gardens, and the future Pope breathed the high air of the Quirinal hill with a sense of relief, and dreamed of living up there, far above the city, literally in an atmosphere of his own. Therefore, when he was Pope, he made the great palace that crowns the eminence, completing and extending a much smaller building planned by the wise183 Gregory the Thirteenth, and ever since then, until , the Popes lived there during some part of the year. It is modern, as age is reckoned in Rome, and it has modern associations in the memory of living men.

It was from the great balcony of the Quirinal that Pius the Ninth pronounced his famous benediction to an enthusiastic and patriotic multitude in . It will be remembered that a month after his election, Pius proclaimed a general amnesty in favour of all persons imprisoned for political crimes, and a decree by which all criminal prosecutions for political offences should be immediately discontinued, unless the persons accused were ecclesiastics, soldiers, or servants of the government, or criminals in the universal sense of the word.

The announcement was received with a frenzy of enthusiasm, and Rome went mad with delight. Instinctively, the people began to move towards the Quirinal from all parts of the city, as soon as the proclamation was published; the stragglers became a band, and swelled to a crowd; music was heard, flags appeared and the crowd swelled to a multitude that thronged the streets, singing, cheering and shouting for joy as they pushed their way up to the palace, filling the square, the streets that led to it and the Via della Dateria below it, to overflowing. In answer to this popular demonstration the Pope appeared upon the great balcony above the main entrance; a shout louder than all the rest burst from below, the long drawn 'Viva!' of184 the southern races; he lifted his hand, and there was silence; and in the calm summer air his quiet eyes were raised towards the sky as he imparted his benediction to the people of Rome.

Twenty-four years later, when the Italians had taken Rome, a detachment of soldiers accompanied by a smith and his assistants marched up to the same gate. Not a soul was within, and they had instructions to enter and take possession of the palace. In the presence of a small and silent crowd of sullen-looking men of the people, the doors were forced.

The difference between Unity under Augustus and Unity under Victor Emmanuel is that under the Empire the Romans took Italy, whereas under the Kingdom the Italians have taken Rome. Without pretending that there can be any moral distinction between the two, one may safely admit that there is a great and vital one between the two conditions of Rome, at the two periods of history, a distinction no less than that which separates the conqueror from the conquered, and the fruits of conquest from the consequences of subjection. But thinking men do not forget that they look at the past in one way and at the present in another; and that while the actions of a nation are dictated by the impulses of contagious sentiment, the judgments of history are too often based upon an all but commercial reckoning and balancing of profit and loss.

When Sixtus the Fifth was building the Quirinal185 palace, he was not working in a wilderness resembling the deserted fields of the outlying Monti. The hill was covered with gardens and villas. Ippolito d'Este, the son of Alfonso, Duke of Ferrara, and of Lucrezia Borgia, had built himself a residence on the west side of the hill, surrounded by gardens. It was in the manner of his magnificent palace at Tivoli, that Villa d'Este of which the melancholy charm had such a mysterious attraction for Liszt, where the dark cypresses reflect their solemn beauty in the stagnant water, and a weed-grown terrace mourns the dead artist in the silence of decay.

PALAZZO DEL QUIRINALE PALAZZO DEL QUIRINALE

Further on, along the Via Venti Settembre, stretched the pleasure grounds of Oliviero, Cardinal Carafa, who is remembered as the man who first recognized the merits of the beautiful mutilated group subsequently known as 'Pasquino,' and set it upon the pedestal which made it famous, and gave its name a place in all languages, by the witty lampoons and stinging satires almost daily affixed to the block of stone. Many other villas followed in the same direction, and in those insecure days not a few Romans, when the summer days grew hot, were content to move up from their palaces in the lower parts of the city to breathe the somewhat better air of the Quirinal and the Esquiline, instead of risking a journey to the country.

Sixtus the Fifth died in the Quirinal palace, and twenty-one other Popes have died there since, all following the curious custom of bequeathing their hearts and viscera to the parish Church of the Saints Vincent and Anastasius, which is known as the Church of Cardinal Mazarin, because the tasteless front was built by him, though the rest existed much earlier. It stands opposite the fountain of Trevi, at one corner of the little square; the vault in which the urns were placed is just behind and below the high altar; but Benedict the Fourteenth built a special monument for them on the left of the apse, and a tablet on the right records the names of the Popes who left these strange legacies to the church.

In passing, one may remember that Mazarin himself was born in the Region of Trevi, the son of a Sicilian,—like Crispi and Rudinì. His father was employed at first as a butler and then as a steward by the Colonna, married an illegitimate daughter of the family, and lived to see his granddaughter, Maria Mancini, married to the head of the house, and his son a cardinal and despot of France, and himself, after the death of his first wife, the honoured husband of

Porzia Orsini, so that he was the only man in history who was married both to an Orsini and to a Colonna. In the light of his father's extraordinary good fortune, the success of the son, though not less great, is at least less astonishing. The magnificent Rospigliosi palace, often ascribed by a mistake to Cardinal Scipio Borghese, was the Palazzo Mazarini and Mazarin's father died there; it was inherited by the Dukes of Nevers, through another niece of the Cardinal's, and was bought from them between and , by Prince Rospigliosi, brother of Pope Clement the Ninth, then reigning.

Urban the Eighth, the Barberini Pope, had already left his mark on the Quirinal hill. The great Barberini palace was built by him, it is said, of stones taken from the Colosseum, whereupon a Pasquinade announced that 'the Barberini had done what the Barbarians had not.' The Barbarians did not pull down the Colosseum, it is true, but they could assuredly not have built as Urban did, and in that particular instance, without188 wishing to justify the vandalisms of the centuries succeeding the Renascence, it may well be asked whether the Amphitheatre is not more picturesque in its half-ruined state, as it stands, and whether the city is not richer by a great work of art in the princely dwelling which faces the street of the Four Fountains.

Among the many memories of the Quirinal there is one more mysterious than the rest. The great Baths of Constantine extended over the site of the Palazzo Rospigliosi, and the ruins were in part standing at the end of the sixteenth century. It is related by a writer of those days and an eye-witness of the fact, that a vault was discovered beneath the old baths, about eighty feet long by twenty wide, closed at one end by a wall thrown up with evident haste and lack of skill, and completely filled with human bodies that fell to dust at the first touch, evidently laid there all at the same time, just after death, and probably numbering at least a thousand. In vain one conjectures the reason of such wholesale burial—one of Nero's massacres, perhaps, or a plague. No one can tell.

The invaluable Baracconi, often quoted, recalls the fact that Tasso, when a child, lived with his father in some house on the Monte Cavallo, when the execrable Carafa cardinal and his brother had temporarily succeeded in seizing all the Colonna property; and he gives a letter of Bernardo, the poet's father, written in July to his wife, who was away just then.

PIAZZA BARBERINI PIAZZA BARBERINI

'I do not wish the children to go to the vineyard because they get too hot, and the air is bad there this summer, but in order that they may have a change, I took steps to have the use of the Boccaccio Vineyard [Villa Colonna, and the

Duke of Paliano [then a Carafa, for the latter had stolen the title as well as the lands has let me have it, and we have been here a week and shall stay all summer in this good air.'

The words call up a picture of Tasso, a small boy, pale with the heat of a Roman summer, but restless and for ever running about, overheated and catching cold like all delicate children, which brings the unhappy poet a little nearer to us.

Of those great villas and gardens there remain the Colonna, the Rospigliosi and the Quirinal, by far the largest of the three, and enclosing between four walls an area almost, if not quite, equal to the Pincio. The great palace where twenty-two popes died is inhabited by the royal family of Italy and crowns the height, as the Vatican, far away across the Tiber, is also on an eminence of its own. They face each other, like two principles in natural and eternal opposition,—Rome the conqueror of the world, and Italy the conqueror of Rome. And he who loves the land for its own sake can only pray that if they must oppose each other for ever in heart, they may abide in that state of civilized though unreconciled peace, which is the nation's last and only hope of prosperity.

REGION III COLONNA

When the present Queen of Italy first came to Rome as Princess Margaret, and drove through the city to obtain a general impression of it, she reached the Piazza Colonna and asked what the column might be which is the most conspicuous landmark in that part of Rome and gives a name to the square, and to the whole Region. The answer of the elderly officer who accompanied the Princess and her ladies is historical. 'That column,' he answered, 'is the Column of Piazza Colonna'—'the Column of Column Square,' as we might say —and that was all he could tell concerning it, for his business was not archæology, but soldiering. The column was erected by the Emperor Marcus Aurelius, whose equestrian statue stands on the Capitol, to commemorate his victory over the Marcomanni.

ARCH OF TITUS ARCH OF TITUS

It is remarkable that so many of the monuments still preserved comparatively intact should have been set up by the adoptive line of the so-called Antonines, from Trajan to Marcus Aurelius, and that the two monster columns, the one in Piazza Colonna and the one in Trajan's Forum, should be the work of the last and the first of those emperors, respectively. Among other memorials of them are the Colosseum, the Arch of Titus and the statue mentioned above. The lofty Septizonium is levelled to the ground, the Palaces of the Cæsars are a mountain of ruins, the triumphal arches of Marcus Aurelius and of Domitian have disappeared with those of Gratian, of Valens, of192 Arcadius and of many others; but the two gigantic columns still stand erect with their sculptured tales of victory and triumph almost unbroken, surmounted by the statues of Saint Peter and Saint Paul, whose memory was sacred to all Christians long before the monuments were erected, and to whom, respectively, they have been dedicated by a later age.

There may have been a connection, too, in the minds of the people, between the 'Column of Piazza Colonna' and the Column of the Colonna family, since a great part of this Region had fallen under the domination of the noble house, and was held by them with a chain of towers and fortifications; but the pillar which is the device of the Region terminates in the statue of the Apostle Peter, whereas the one which figures in the shield of Colonna is crowned with a royal crown, in memory of the coronation of Lewis the Bavarian by Sciarra, who himself generally lived in a palace facing the small square which bears his name, and which is only a widening of the Corso just north of San Marcello, the scene of Jacopo Colonna's brave protest against his kinsman's mistaken imperialism.

The straight Corso itself, or what is the most important part of it to Romans, runs through the Region from San Lorenzo in Lucina to Piazza di Sciarra, and beyond that, southwards, it forms the western boundary of Trevi as far as the Palazzo di Venezia, and the Ripresa de' Barberi—the 'Catching of the Racers.' West of the193 Corso, the Region takes in the Monte Citorio and the Piazza of the Pantheon, but not the Pantheon itself, and eastwards it embraces the new quarter which was formerly the Villa Ludovisi, and follows the Aurelian wall, from Porta Salaria to Porta Pinciana. Corso means a 'course,' and the Venetian Paul the Second, who found Rome dull compared with Venice, gave it the name when he made it a race-course for the Carnival, towards the close of the fifteenth century. Before that it was Via Lata,—'Broad Street,'—and was a straight continuation of the Via Flaminia, the main northern highway from the city. For centuries it has been the chief playground of the Roman Carnival, a festival of which, perhaps, nothing but the memory will remain in a few years, when the world will wonder how it could be possible that the population of the grave old city should have gone mad each year for ten days and behaved itself by day and night like a crowd of schoolboys let loose.

'Carnival' is supposed to be derived from 'Carnelevamen,' a 'solace for the flesh.' Byron alone is responsible for the barbarous derivation 'Carne Vale,' farewell meat—a philological impossibility. In the minds of the people it is probably most often translated as 'Meat Time,' a name which had full meaning in times when occasional strict fasting and frequent abstinence were imposed on Romans almost by law. Its beginnings are lost in the dawnless night of time —of 194 Time, who was Kronos, of Kronos who was Saturn, of Saturn who gave his mysterious name to the Saturnalia in which Carnival had its origin. His temple stood at the foot of the Capitol hill, facing the corner of the Forum, and there are remains of it today, tall columns in a row, with architrave and frieze and cornice; from the golden milestone close at hand, as from the beginning of time, were measured the ways of the world to the ends of the earth; and the rites performed within it were older than any others, and different, for here the pious Roman worshipped with uncovered head, whereas in all other temples he drew up his robes as a veil lest any sight of evil omen should meet his eyes, and here waxen tapers were first burned in Rome in honour of a god. And those same tapers played a part, to the end, on the last night of Carnival. But in the coincidence of old feasts with new ones, the festival of Lupercus falls nearer to the time of Ash Wednesday, for the Lupercalia were celebrated on the fifteenth of February, whereas the Carnival of Saturn began on the seventeenth of December.

Lupercus was but a little god, yet he was great among the shepherds in Rome's pastoral beginnings, for he was the driver away of wolves, and on his day the early settlers ran round and round their sheepfold on the Palatine, all dressed in skins of fresh-slain goats, praising the Faun god, and calling upon him to protect their flocks. And in truth, as the winter, when wolves are 195 hungry and daring, was over, his protection was a foregone conclusion till the cold days came again. The grotto dedicated to him was on the northwest slope of the Palatine, nearly opposite the Church of Saint George in Velabro, across the Via di San Teodoro; and all that remains of the great festival in which Mark Antony and the rest ran like wild men through the streets of Rome, smiting men and women with the purifying leathern thong, and offering at last that crown which Cæsar thrice refused, is merged and forgotten, with the Saturnalia, in the ten days' feasting and rioting that change to the ashes and sadness of Lent, as the darkest night follows the brightest day. For the Romans always loved strong contrasts.

Carnival, in the wider sense, begins at Christmas and ends when Lent begins; but to most people it means but the last ten days of the season, when festivities crowd upon each other till pleasure fights for minutes as for jewels; when tables are spread all night and lights are put out at dawn; when society dances itself into distraction and poor men make such feasting as they can; when no one works who can help it, and no work done is worth having, because it is done for double price and half its value; when affairs of love are hastened to solution or catastrophe, and affairs of state are treated with the scorn they merit in the eyes of youth, because the only sense is laughter, and the only wisdom, folly. That is Carnival, personified by the people as a riotous old red-cheeked, bottle-nosed hunchback, animated by the spirit of fun.

In a still closer sense, Carnival is the Carnival in the Corso, or was; for it is dead beyond resuscitation, and such efforts as are made to give it life again are but foolish incantations that call up sad ghosts of joy, spiritless and witless. But within living memory, it was very different. In those days which can never come back, the Corso was a sight to see and not to be forgotten. The small citizens who had small houses in the street let every window to the topmost story for the whole ten days; the rich whose palaces faced the favoured line threw open their doors to their friends; every window was decorated, from every balcony gorgeous hangings, or rich carpets, or even richer tapestries hung down; the street was strewn thick with yellow sand, and wheresoever there was an open space wooden seats were built up, row above row, where one might hire a place to see the show and join in throwing flowers, and the lime-covered 'confetti' that stung like small shot and whitened everything like meal, and forced everyone in the street or within reach of it to wear a shield of thin wire netting to guard the face, and thick gloves to shield the hands; or, in older times, a mask, black, white, or red, or modelled and painted with extravagant features, like evil beings in a dream.

TWIN CHURCHES AT THE ENTRANCE TO THE CORSO TWIN CHURCHES AT THE ENTRANCE TO THE CORSO

From a print of the last century
In the early afternoon of each day except Sunday it all began, day after day the same, save that the fun grew wilder and often rougher as the doom of Ash Wednesday drew near. First when the people had gathered in their places, high and low, and already thronged the street from side to side, there was a distant rattle of scabbards and a thunder of hoofs, and all fell back, crowding and climbing upon one another, to let a score of cavalrymen trot through, clearing the way for the carriages of the 'Senator' and Municipality, which drove from end to end of the Corso with their scarlet and yellow liveries, before any other vehicles were allowed to pass, or any pelting with 'confetti' began. But on the instant when they had gone by, the showers began, right, left, upwards, downwards, like little storms of flowers and snow in the afternoon sunshine, and the whole air was filled with the laughter and laughing chatter of twenty thousand men and women and children—such a sound as could be heard nowhere else in the world. Many have heard a great host cheer, many have heard the battle-cries of armies, many have heard the terrible deep yell that goes up from an angry multitude in times of revolution; but only those who remember the Carnival as it used to be have heard a whole city laugh, and the memory is worth having, for it is like no other. The sound used to flow along

in great waves, following the sights that passed, and swelling with them to a peal that was like a cheer, and ebbing then to a steady, even ripple of enjoyment that never ceased till it rose again in sheer joy of something new to see. Nothing can give an idea of the picture in times when Rome was still Roman; no power of description can call up the crowd that thronged and jammed the long, narrow street, till the slowly moving carriages and cars seemed to force their way through the stiffly packed mass of humanity as a strong vessel ploughs her course up-stream through packed ice in winter. Yet no one was hurt, and an order reigned which could never have been produced by any means except the most thorough good temper and the determination of each individual to do no harm to his neighbour, though all respect of individuals199 was as completely gone as in any anarchy of revolution. The more respectable a man looked who ventured into the press in ordinary clothes, the more certainly he became at once the general mark for hail-storms of 'confetti.' No uniform nor distinguishing badge was respected, excepting those of the squad of cavalrymen who cleared the way, and the liveries of the Municipality's coaches. Men and women were travestied and disguised in every conceivable way, as Punch and Judy, as judges and lawyers with enormous square black caps, black robes and bands, or in dresses of the eighteenth century, or as Harlequins, or even as bears and monkeys, singly, or in twos and threes, or in little companies of fifteen or twenty, all dressed precisely alike and performing comic evolutions with military exactness. Everyone carried a capacious pouch, or a fishing-basket, or some receptacle of the kind for the white 'confetti,' and arms and hands were ceaselessly swung in air, flinging vast quantities of the snowy stuff at long range and short. At every corner and in every side street, men sold it out of huge baskets, by the five, and ten, and twenty pounds, weighing it out with the ancient steelyard balance. Every balcony was lined with long troughs of it, constantly replenished by the house servants; every carriage and car had a full supply. And through all the air the odd, clean odour of the fresh plaster mingled with the fragrance of the box-leaves and the200 perfume of countless flowers. For flowers were thrown, too, in every way, loose and scattered, or in hard little bunches, the 'mazzetti,' that almost hurt when they struck the mark, and in beautiful nosegays, rarely flung at random when a pretty face was within sight at a window. The cars, often charmingly decorated, were filled with men and women representing some period of fashion, or some incident in history, or some allegorical subject, and were sometimes two or three stories high, and covered all over with garlands of flowers and box and myrtle. In the intervals between them endless open carriages moved along, lined with white, filled with white dominos, drawn by horses all protected and covered with white cotton robes, against the whiter 'confetti'—everyone fighting mock battles with everyone else, till it seemed impossible that anything could be left to throw, and the long perspective of the narrow street grew dim between the high palaces, and misty and purple in the evening light.

A gun fired somewhere far away as a signal warned the carriages to turn out, and make way for the race that was to follow. The last moments were the hottest and the wildest, as flowers, 'confetti,' sugar plums with comet-like tails, wreaths, garlands, everything, went flying through the air in a final and reckless profusion, and as the last car rolled away the laughter and shouting ceased, and all was hushed in the expectation of201 the day's last sight. Again, the clatter of hoofs and scabbards, as the dragoons cleared the way; twenty thousand heads and necks craning to look northward, as the people pushed back to the side pavements; silence, and the inevitable yellow dog that haunts all race-courses, scampering over the white street, scared by the shouts, and catcalls, and bursts of spasmodic laughter; then a far sound of flying hoofs, a dead silence, and the quick breathing of suppressed excitement; louder and louder the hoofs, deader the hush; and then, in the dash of a second, in the scud of a storm, in a whirlwind of light and colour and sparkling gold leaf, with straining necks, and flashing eyes, and wide red nostrils flecked with foam, the racing colts flew by as fleet as darting lightning, riderless and swift as rock-swallows by the sea.

Then, if it were the last night of Carnival, as the purple air grew brown in the dusk, myriads of those wax tapers first used in Saturn's temple of old lit up the street like magic and the last game of all began, for every man and woman and child strove to put out another's candle, and the long, laughing cry, 'No taper! No taper! Senza moccolo!' went ringing up to the darkling sky. Long canes with cloths or damp sponges or extinguishers fixed to them started up from nowhere, down from everywhere, from window and balcony to the street below, and from the street to the low balconies above. Put out at every instant, the little candles were instantly relighted, till they were consumed down to the hand; and as they burned low, another cry went up, 'Carnival is dead! Carnival is dead!' But he was not really dead till midnight, when the last play of the season had been acted in the playhouses, the last dance danced, the last feast eaten amid song and laughter, and the solemn Patarina of the Capitol tolled out the midnight warning like a funeral knell. That was the end.

The riderless race was at least four hundred years old when it was given up. The horses were always called Bárberi, with the accent on the first syllable, and there has been much discussion about the origin of the name. Some say that it meant horses from Barbary, but then it should be pronounced Barbéri, accented on the penultimate. Others think it stood for Bárbari—barbarian, that is, unridden. The Romans never misplace an accent, and rarely mistake the proper quantity of a syllable long or short. For my own part, though no scholar has as yet suggested it, I believe that the common people, always fond of easy witticisms and catchwords, coined the appellation, with an eye to the meaning of both the other derivations, out of Barbo, the family name of Pope Paul the Second, who first instituted the Carnival races, and set the winning post under the balcony of the huge Palazzo di Venezia, which he had built beside the Church of Saint Mark, to the honour and glory of his native city.

He made men run foot-races, too: men, youths and boys, of all ages; and the poor Jews, in heavy cloth garments, were first fed and stuffed with cakes and then made to run, too. The jests of the Middle Age were savage compared with the roughest play of later times.

The pictures of old Rome are fading fast. I can remember, when a little boy, seeing the great Carnival of , when the Prince of Wales was in Rome, and the masks which had been forbidden since the revolution were allowed again in his honour; and before the flower throwing began, I saw Liszt, the pianist, not yet in orders, but dressed in a close-fitting and very fashionable grey frock-coat, with a grey high hat, young then, tall, athletic and erect; he came out suddenly from a doorway, looked to the right and left in evident fear of being made a mark for 'confetti,' crossed the street hurriedly and disappeared—not at all the silver-haired, priestly figure the world knew so well in later days. And by and by the Prince of Wales came by in a simple open carriage, a thin young man in a black coat, with a pale, face and a quiet smile, looking all about him with an almost boyish interest, and bowing to the right and left.

Then in deep contrast of sadness, out of the past years comes a great funeral by night, down the Corso; hundreds of brown, white-bearded friars, two and two with huge wax candles, singing the ancient chant of204 the penitential psalms; hundreds of hooded lay brethren of the Confraternities, some in black, some in white, with round holes for their eyes that flashed through, now and then, in the yellow glare of the flaming tapers; hundreds of little street boys beside them in the shadow, holding up big horns of grocers' paper to catch the dripping wax; and then, among priests in cotta and stole, the open bier carried on men's shoulders, and on it the peaceful figure of a dead girl, white-robed, blossom crowned, delicate as a frozen flower in the cold winter air. She had died of an innocent love, they said, and she was borne in through the gates of the Santi Apostoli to her rest in the solemn darkness. Nor has anyone been buried in that way since then.

SAN LORENZO IN LUCINA SAN LORENZO IN LUCINA

In the days of Paul the Second, what might be called living Rome, taken in the direction of the Corso, began at the Arch of Marcus Aurelius, long attributed to Domitian, which stood at the corner of the small square called after San Lorenzo in Lucina. Beyond that point, northwards and eastwards, the city was a mere desert, and on the west side the dwelling-houses fell away towards the Mausoleum of Augustus, the fortress of the Colonna. The arch itself used to be called the Arch of Portugal, because a Portuguese Cardinal, Giovanni da Costa, lived in the Fiano palace at the corner of the Corso. No one would suppose that very modern-looking building, with its smooth front and conventional balconies, to be six hundred years old, the ancient habitation of all the successive Cardinals of Saint Lawrence. Its only other interest, perhaps, lies in the fact that it formed part of the great estates bestowed by Sixtus the Fifth on his nephews, and was nevertheless sold over their children's heads for debt, fifty-five years after his death. The swineherd's race was prodigal, excepting the 'Great Friar' himself, and, like the Prodigal Son, it was not long before the Peretti were reduced to eating the husks.

It was natural that the palaces of the Renascence should rise along the only straight street of any length in what was then the inhabited part of the city, and206 that the great old Roman Barons, the Colonna, the Orsini, the Caetani, should continue to live in their strongholds, where they had always dwelt. The Caetani, indeed, once bought from a Florentine banker what is now the Ruspoli palace, and Sciarra Colonna had lived far down the Corso; but with these two exceptions, the princely habitations between the Piazza del Popolo and the Piazza di Venezia are almost all the property of families once thought foreigners in Rome. The greatest, the most magnificent private dwelling in the world is the Doria Pamfili palace, as the Doria themselves were the most famous, and became the most powerful of those many nobles who, in the course of centuries, settled in the capital and became Romans, not only in name but in fact—Doria, Borghese, Rospigliosi, Pallavicini and others of less enduring fame or reputation, who came in the train or alliance of a Pope, and remained in virtue of accumulated riches and acquired honour.

Two hundred and fifty years have passed since a council of learned doctors and casuists decided for Pope Innocent the Tenth the precise limit of his just power to enrich his nephews and relations, the Pamfili, by an alliance with whom the original Doria of Genoa added another name to their own, and inherited the vast estates. But nearly four hundred years before Innocent, the Doria had been high admirals and almost despots of Genoa. For they were a race of seamen207 from the first, in a republic where seamanship was the first essential to distinction. Albert Doria overcame the Pisans off Meloria in , slaying five thousand, and taking eleven thousand prisoners. Conrad, his son, was 'Captain of the Genoese Freedom,' and 'Captain of the People.' Lamba Doria vanquished the Venetians under the brave Andrea Dandolo, and Paganino Doria conquered them again under another Andrea Dandolo; and then an Andrea Doria took service with the Pope, and became the greatest sailor in Europe, the hero of a hundred sea-fights, at one time the ally of Francis the First of France, and the most dangerous opponent of Gonzalvo da Cordova, then high admiral of the Empire under Charles the Fifth, a destroyer of pirates, by turns the idol, the enemy and the despot of his own city, Genoa, and altogether such a type of a soldier-sailor of fortune as the world has not seen before or since. And there were others after him, notably Gian Andrea Doria, remembered by the great victory over the Turks at Lepanto, whence he brought home those gorgeous Eastern spoils of tapestry and embroideries which hang in the Doria palace today.

PALAZZO DORIA PAMFILI PALAZZO DORIA PAMFILI

The history of the palace itself is not without interest, for it shows how property, which was not in the possession of the original Barons, sometimes passed from hand to hand, changing names with each new owner, in the rise and fall of fortunes in those times. The first building seems to have belonged to the Chapter of Santa Maria Maggiore, which somehow ceded it to Cardinal Santorio, who spent an immense sum in rebuilding, extending and beautifying it. When it was almost finished, Julius the Second came to see it, and after expressing the highest admiration for the work, observed that such a habitation was less fitting for a prince of the church than for a secular duke—meaning, by the latter, his own nephew, Francesco della Rovere, then Duke of Urbino; and the unfortunate Santorio, who had succeeded in preserving his possessions under the domination of the Borgia, was forced to209 offer the most splendid palace in Rome as a gift to the person designated by his master. He died of a broken heart within the year. A hundred years later, the Florentine Aldobrandini, nephew of Clement the Eighth, bought it from the Dukes of Urbino for twelve thousand measures of grain, furnished them for the purpose by their uncle, and finally, when it had fallen in inheritance to Donna Olimpia Aldobrandini, Innocent the Tenth married her to his nephew, Camillo Pamfili, from whom, by the fusion of the two families, it at last came into the hands of the Doria-Pamfili.

The Doria palace is almost two-thirds of the size of Saint Peter's, and within the ground plan of Saint Peter's the Colosseum could stand. It used to be said that a thousand persons lived under the roof outside of the gallery and the private apartments, which alone surpass in extent the majority of royal residences. Without some such comparison mere words can convey nothing to a mind unaccustomed to such size and space, and when the idea is grasped, one asks, naturally enough, how the people lived who built such houses—the people whose heirs, far reduced in splendour, if not in fortune, are driven to let four-fifths of their family mansion, because they find it impossible to occupy more rooms than suffice the Emperor of Germany or the Queen of England. One often hears foreign visitors, ignorant of the real size of palaces in Rome, observe, with contempt, that the Roman princes 'let their palaces.'210 It would be more reasonable to inquire what use could be made of such buildings, if they were not let, or how any family could be expected to inhabit a thousand rooms, and, ultimately, for what purpose such monstrous residences were ever built at all.

The first thing that suggests itself in answer to the latter question as the cause of such boundless extravagance is the inherited giantism of the Latins, to which reference has been more than once made in these pages, and to which the existence of many of the principal buildings in Rome must be ascribed. Next, we may consider that at one time or another, each of the greater Roman palaces has been, in all essentials, the court of a pope or of a reigning feudal prince. Lastly, it must be remembered that each palace was the seat of management of all its owner's estates, and that such administration in those times required a number of scribes and an amount of labour altogether out of proportion with the income derived from the land.

At first sight the study of Italian life in the Middle Age does not seem very difficult, because it is so interesting. But when one has read the old chronicles that have survived, and the histories of those times, one is amazed to see how much we are told about people and their actions, and how very little about the way in which people lived. It is easier to learn the habits of the Egyptians, or the Greeks, or the ancient Romans, or the Assyrians, than to get211 at the daily life of an Italian family between the eleventh and the thirteenth centuries, from such books as we have. There are two reasons for this. One is the scarcity of literature, excepting historical chronicles, until the time of Boccaccio and the Italian storytellers. The other is the fact that what we call the Middle Age was an age of transition from barbarism to the civilization of the Renascence, and the Renascence was reached by sweeping away all the barbarous things that had gone before it.

One must have lived a lifetime in Italy to be able to call up a fairly vivid picture of the eleventh, twelfth, or thirteenth centuries. One must have actually seen the grand old castles and gloomy monasteries, and feudal villages of Calabria and Sicily, where all things are least changed from what they were, and one should understand something of the nature of the Italian people, where the original people have survived; one must try also to realize the violence of those passions which are ugly excrescences on Italian character even now, and which were once the main movers of that character.

There are extant many inventories of lordly residences of earlier times in Italy, for the inventory was taken every time the property changed hands by inheritance or sale. Everyone of these inventories begins at the main gate of the stronghold, and the first item is 'Rope for giving the cord.' Now 'to give the cord'212 was a torture, and all feudal lords had the right to inflict it. The victim's hands were tied behind his back, the rope was made fast to his bound wrists, and he was hoisted some twenty feet or so to the heavy iron ring which is fixed in the middle of the arch of every old Italian castle gateway; he was then allowed to drop suddenly till his feet, to which heavy weights were sometimes attached, were a few inches from the ground, so that the strain of his whole weight fell upon his arms, twisted them backwards, and generally dislocated them at the shoulders. And this was usually done three times, and sometimes twenty times, in succession, to the same prisoner, either as a punishment or by way of examination, to extract a confession of the truth. As the rope of torture was permanently rove through the pulley over the front door, it must have been impossible not to see it and remember what it meant every time one went in or out. And such quick reminders of danger and torture, and sudden, painful death, give the pitch and key of daily existence in the Middle Age. Every man's life was in his hand until it was in his enemy's. Every man might be forced, at a moment's notice, to defend not only his honour, and his belongings, and his life, but his women and children, too,— not against public enemies only, but far more often against private spite and personal hatred. Nowadays, when most men only stake their money on their convictions, it is hard213 to realize how men reasoned who staked their lives at every turn; or to guess, for instance, at what women felt whose husbands and sons, going out for a stroll of an afternoon, in the streets of Rome, might as likely as not be brought home dead of a dozen sword-wounds before evening. A husband, a father, was stabbed in the dark by treachery; try and imagine the daily and year-long sensations of the widowed mother, bringing up her only son deliberately to kill her husband's murderer; teaching him to look upon vengeance as the first, most real and most honourable aim of life, from the time he was old enough to speak, to the time when he should be strong enough to kill. Everything was earnest then. One should remember that most of the stories told by Boccaccio, Sacchetti and Bandello—the stories from which Shakespeare got his Italian plays, his Romeo and Juliet, his Merchant of Venice—were not inventions, but were founded on the truth. Everyone has read about Cæsar Borgia, his murders, his treacheries and his end, and he is held up to us as a type of monstrous wickedness. But a learned Frenchman, Émile Gebhart, has recently written a rather convincing treatise, to show that Cæsar Borgia was not a monster at all, nor even much of an exception to the general rule among the Italian despots of his day, and his day was civilized compared with that of Rienzi, of Boniface the Eighth, of Sciarra Colonna.

In order to understand anything about the real life of the Middle Age, one should begin at the beginning; one should see the dwellings, the castles, and the palaces with their furniture and arrangements, one should realize the stern necessities as well as the few luxuries of that time. And one should make acquaintance with the people themselves, from the grey-haired old baron, the head of the house, down to the scullery man and the cellarer's boy and the stable lads. And then, knowing something of the people and their homes, one might begin to learn something about their household occupations, their tremendously tragic interests and their few and simple amusements.

PORTA SAN LORENZO PORTA SAN LORENZO

The first thing that strikes one about the dwellings is the enormous strength of those that remain. The main idea, in those days, when a man built a house, was to fortify himself and his belongings against attacks from the outside, and every other consideration was secondary to that. That is true not only of the Barons' castles in the country and of their fortified palaces in town,—which were castles, too, for that matter,—but of the dwellings of all classes of people who could afford to live independently, that is, who were not serfs and retainers of the rich. We talk of fire-proof buildings nowadays, which are mere shells of iron and brick and stone that shrivel up like writing-paper in a great fire. The only really fire-proof buildings were those of the Middle Age, which consisted of nothing but stone and mortar throughout, stone walls, stone vaults, stone floors, and often stone tables and stone seats. I once visited the ancient castle of Muro, in the Basilicata, one of the southern provinces in Italy, where Queen Joanna the First paid her life for her sins at last, and died under the feather pillow that was forced down upon her face by two Hungarian soldiers. It is as wild and lonely a place as you will meet with in Europe, and yet the great castle has never been a ruin, nor at any time uninhabited, since it was built in the eleventh century, over eight hundred years ago. Nor has the lower part of it ever needed repair. The walls are in places twenty-five feet thick, of solid stone and mortar, so that the embrasure by which each narrow window is reached is like a tunnel cut through rock, while the deep prisons below are hewn out of the rock itself. Up to what we should call the third story, every room is vaulted. Above that the floors are laid on beams, and the walls are not more than eight feet thick—comparatively flimsy for such a place! Nine-tenths of it was built for strength—the small remainder for comfort; there is not a single large hall in all the great fortress, and the courtyard within the main gate is a gloomy, ill-shaped little paved space, barely big enough to give fifty men standing room. Nothing can give any idea of the crookedness of it all, of the small dark corridors, the narrow winding steps, the dusky inclined ascents, paved with broad flagstones that echo216 the lightest tread, and that must have rung and roared like sea caves to the tramp of armed men. And so it was in the cities, too. In Rome, bits of the old strongholds survive still. There were more of them thirty years ago. Even the more modern palaces of the late Renascence are built in such a way that they must have afforded a safe refuge against everything except artillery. The strong iron-studded doors and the heavily grated windows of the ground floor would stand a siege from the street. The Palazzo Gabrielli, for two or three centuries the chief dwelling of the Orsini, is built in the midst of the city like a great fortification, with escarpments and buttresses and loop-holes; and at the main gate there is still a portcullis which sinks into the ground by a system of chains and balance weights and is kept in working order even now.

In the Middle Age, each town palace had one or more towers, tall, square and solid, which were used as lookouts and as a refuge in case the rest of the palace should be taken by an enemy. The general principle of all mediæval towers was that they were entered through a small window at a great height above the ground, by means of a jointed wooden ladder. Once inside, the people drew the ladder up after them and took it in with them, in separate pieces. When that was done, they were comparatively safe, before the age of gunpowder. There were no windows to break, it was impossible to get in, and the besieged party217 could easily keep anyone from scaling the tower, by pouring boiling oil or melted lead from above, or with stones and missiles, so that as long as provisions and water held out, the besiegers could do nothing. As for water, the great rainwater cistern was always in the foundations of the tower itself, immediately under the prison, which got neither light nor air excepting from a hole in the floor above. Walls from fifteen to twenty feet thick could not be battered down with any engines then in existence. Altogether, the tower was a safe place in times of danger. It is said that at one time there were over four hundred of these in Rome, belonging to the nobles, great and small.

The small class of well-to-do commoners, the merchants and goldsmiths, such as they were, who stood between the nobles and the poor people, imitated the nobles as much as they could, and strengthened their houses by every means. For their dwellings were their warehouses, and in times of disturbance the first instinct of the people was to rob the merchants, unless they chanced to be strong enough to rob the nobles, as sometimes happened. But in Rome the merchants were few, and were very generally retainers or dependants of the great houses. It is frequent in the chronicles to find a man mentioned as the 'merchant' of the Colonna family, or of the Orsini, or of one of the independent Italian princes, like the Duke of Urbino. Such a man acted as agent to sell the218 produce of a great estate; part of his business was to lend money to the owner, and he also imported from abroad the scanty merchandise which could be imported at all. About half of it usually fell into the hands of highwaymen before it reached the city, and the price of luxuries was proportionately high. Such men, of course, lived well, though there was a wide difference between their mode of life and that of the nobles, not so much in matters of abundance and luxury, as in principle. The chief rule was that the wives and daughters of the middle class did a certain amount of housekeeping work, whereas the wives and daughters of the nobles did not. The burgher's wife kept house herself, overlooked the cooking, and sometimes cooked a choice dish with her own hands, and taught her daughters to do so. A merchant might have a considerable retinue of men, for his service and protection, and they carried staves when they accompanied their master abroad, and lanterns at night. But the baron's men were men-at-arms,—practically soldiers,—who wore his colours, and carried swords and pikes, and lit the way for their lord at night with torches, always the privilege of the nobles. As a matter of fact, they were generally the most dangerous cutthroats whom the nobleman was able to engage, highwaymen, brigands and outlaws, whom he protected against the semblance of the law; whereas the merchant's train[219] consisted of honest men who worked for him in his warehouse, or they were countrymen from his farms, if he had any.

It is not easy to give any adequate idea of those great mediæval establishments, except by their analogy with the later ones that came after them. They were enormous in extent, and singularly uncomfortable in their internal arrangement.

A curious book, published in , and therefore at the first culmination of the Renascence, has lately been reprinted. It is entitled 'Concerning the management of a Roman Nobleman's Court,' and was dedicated to 'The magnificent and Honourable Messer Cola da Benevento,' forty years after the death of the Borgia Pope and during the reign of Paul the Third, Farnese, who granted the writer a copyright for ten years. The little volume is full of interesting details, and the attendant gentlemen and servants enumerated give some idea of what according to the author was not considered extravagant for a nobleman of the sixteenth century. There were to be two chief chamberlains, a general controller of the estates, a chief steward, four chaplains, a master of the horse, a private secretary and an assistant secretary, an auditor, a lawyer and four literary personages, 'Letterati,' who, among them, must know 'the four principal languages of the world, namely, Hebrew, Greek, Latin and Italian.' The omission of every other living language[220] but the latter, when Francis the First, Charles the Fifth and Henry the Eighth were reigning, is pristinely Roman in its contempt of 'barbarians.' There were also to be six gentlemen of the chambers, a private master of the table, a chief carver and ten waiting men, a butler of the pantry with an assistant, a butler of the wines, six head grooms, a marketer with an assistant, a storekeeper, a cellarer, a carver for the serving gentlemen, a chief cook, an under cook and assistant, a chief scullery man, a water carrier, a sweeper,—and last in the list, a physician, whom the author puts at the end of the list, 'not because a doctor is not worthy of honour, but in order not to seem to expect any infirmity for his lordship or his household.'

This was considered a 'sufficient household' for a nobleman, but by no means an extravagant one, and many of the officials enumerated were provided with one or more servants, while no mention is made of any ladies in the establishment nor of the numerous retinue they required. But one remembers the six thousand servants of Augustus, all honourably buried in one place, and the six hundred who waited on Livia alone; and the modest one hundred and seven which were reckoned 'sufficient' for the Lord Cola of Benevento sink into comparative insignificance. For Livia, besides endless keepers of her robes and folders of her clothes—a special office—and hairdressers, perfumers, jewellers and shoe keepers, had a special 221 adorner of her ears, a keeper of her chair and a governess for her favourite lap-dog.

The little book contains the most complete details concerning daily expenditure for food and drink for the head of the house and his numerous gentlemen, which amounted in a year to the really not extravagant sum of four thousand scudi, or dollars, over fourteen hundred being spent on wine alone. The allowance was a jug—rather more than a quart—of pure wine daily to each of the 'gentlemen,' and the same measure diluted with one-third of water to all the rest. Sixteen ounces of beef, mutton, or veal were reckoned for every person, and each received twenty ounces of bread of more or less fine quality, according to his station; and an average of twenty scudi was allowed daily as given away in charity,—which was not ungenerous, either, for such a household. The olive oil used for the table and for lamps was the same, and was measured together, and the household received each a pound of cheese, monthly, besides a multitude of other eatables, all of which are carefully enumerated and valued. Among other items of a different nature are 'four or five large wax candles daily, for his lordship,' and wax for torches 'to accompany the dishes brought to his table, and to accompany his lordship and the gentlemen out of doors at night,' and 'candles for the altar,' and tallow candles for use about the house. As for salaries and wages, the controller and chief steward received 222 ten scudi, each month, whereas the chaplain only got two, and the 'literary men,' who were expected to know Hebrew, Greek and Latin, were each paid one hundred scudi yearly. The physician was required to be not only 'learned, faithful, diligent and affectionate,' but also 'fortunate' in his profession. Considering the medical practices of those days, a doctor could certainly not hope to heal his patients without the element of luck.

The old-fashioned Roman character is careful, if not avaricious, with occasional flashes of astonishing extravagance, and its idea of riches is so closely associated with that of power as to make the display of a numerous retinue its first and most congenial means of exhibiting great wealth; so that to this day a Roman in reduced fortune will live very poorly before he will consent to exist without the two or three superfluous footmen who loiter all day in his hall, or the handsome equipage in which his wife and daughters are accustomed to take the daily drive, called from ancient times the 'trottata,' or 'trot,' in the Villa Borghese, or the Corso, or on the Pincio, and gravely provided for in the terms of the marriage contract. At a period when servants were necessary, not only for show but also for personal protection, it is not surprising that the nobles should have kept an extravagant number of them.

PALAZZO DI MONTE CITORIO PALAZZO DI MONTE CITORIO

From a print of the last century
Then also, to account for the size of Roman palaces, there was the patriarchal system of life, now rapidly falling into disuse. The so-called 'noble floor' of every mansion is supposed to be reserved exclusively for the father and mother of the family, and the order of arranging the rooms is as much a matter of rigid rule as in the houses of the ancient Romans, where the vestibule preceded the atrium, the atrium the peristyle, and the latter the last rooms which looked upon the garden. So in the later palace, the door from the first landing of the grand staircase opens upon an outer hall, uncarpeted, but crossed by a strip of matting, and furnished only with a huge table and old-fashioned chests, made with high backs, on which are painted or carved the arms of the family. Here, at least two or three footmen are supposed to be in perpetual readiness to answer the door, the lineally descended representatives of the224 armed footmen who lounged there four hundred years ago. Next to the hall comes the antechamber, sometimes followed by a second, and here is erected the 'baldacchino,' the coloured canopy which marks the privilege of the sixty 'conscript families' of Rome, who rank as princes. It recalls the times when, having powers of justice, and of life and death, the lords sat in state under the overhanging silks, embroidered with their coats of arms, to administer the law. Beyond the antechamber comes the long succession of state apartments, lofty, ponderously decorated, heavily furnished with old-fashioned gilt or carved chairs that stand symmetrically against the walls, and on the latter are hung pictures, priceless works of old masters beside crude portraits of the last century, often arranged much more with regard to the frames than to the paintings. Stiff-legged pier-tables of marble and alabaster face the windows or are placed between them; thick curtains that can be drawn quite back cover the doors; strips of hemp carpet lead straight from one door

to another; the light is dim and cold, half shut out by the window curtains, and gets a peculiar quality of sadness and chilliness, which is essentially characteristic of every old Roman house, where the reception rooms are only intended to be used at night, and the sunny side is exclusively appropriated to the more intimate life of the owners. There may be three, four, six, ten of those big drawing-rooms in succession, each covering about as much space as a small house in New York or London, before one comes to the closed door that gives access to the princess' boudoir, beyond which, generally returning in a direction parallel with the reception rooms, is her bedroom, and the prince's, and the latter's study, and then the private dining-room, the state dining-room, the great ballroom, with clear-story windows, and as many more rooms as the size of the apartment will admit. In the great palaces, the picture gallery takes a whole wing and sometimes two, the library being generally situated on a higher story.

The patriarchal system required that all the married sons, with their wives and children and servants, should be lodged in the same building with their parents. The eldest invariably lived on the second floor, the second son on the third, which is the highest, though there is generally a low rambling attic, occupied by servants, and sometimes by the chaplain, the librarian and the steward, in better rooms. When there were more than two married sons, which hardly ever happened under the old system of primogeniture, they divided the apartments between them as best they could. The unmarried younger children had to put up with what was left. Moreover, in the greatest houses, where there was usually a cardinal of the name, one wing of the first floor was entirely given up to him; and instead of the canopy in the antechamber, flanked by the hereditary coloured umbrellas carried on state occasions by two lackeys behind the family coach, the prince of the Church was entitled to a throne room, as all cardinals are. The eldest son's apartment was generally more or less a repetition of the state one below, but the rooms were lower, the decorations less elaborate, though seldom less stiff in character, and a large part of the available space was given up to the children.

It is clear from all this that even in modern times a large family might take up a great deal of room. Looking back across two or three centuries, therefore, to the days when every princely household was a court, and was called a court, it is easier to understand the existence of such phenomenally vast mansions as the Doria palace, or those of the Borghese, the Altieri, the Barberini and others, who lived in almost royal state, and lodged hundreds upon hundreds of retainers in their homes.

And not only did all the members of the family live under one roof, as a few of them still live, but the custom of dining together at one huge table was universal. A daily dinner of twenty persons—grandparents, parents and children, down to the youngest that is old enough to sit up to its plate in a high chair, would be a serious matter to most European households. But in Rome it was looked upon as a matter of course, and was managed through the steward by a contract with the cook, who was bound to provide a certain number of dishes daily for the fixed meals, but nothing else—not so much as an egg or a slice of toast beyond that. This system still prevails in many households, and as it is to be expected that meals at unusual hours may sometimes be required, an elaborate system of accounts is kept by the steward and his clerks, and the smallest things ordered by any of the sons or daughters are charged against an allowance usually made them, while separate reckonings are kept for the daughters-in-law, for whom certain regular pin-money is provided out of their own dowries at the marriage settlement, all of which goes through the steward's hands. The same settlement, even in recent years, stipulated for a fixed number of dishes of meat daily, generally only two, I believe, for a certain number of new gowns and other clothes, and for a great variety of details, besides the use of a carriage every day, to be harnessed not more than twice, that is, either in the morning and afternoon, or once in the daytime and once at night. Everything,—a cup of tea, a glass of lemonade,—if not mentioned in the marriage settlement, had to be paid for separately. The justice of such an arrangement—for it is just—is only equalled by its inconvenience, for it requires the machinery of a hotel, combined with an honesty not usual in hotels. Undoubtedly, the whole system is directly descended from the practice of the ancients, which made every father of a family the absolute despot of his household, and made it impossible for a son to hold property or have any individual independence during his father's life, and it has not been perceptibly much modified since the Middle Age, until the last few years. Its existence shows in the strongest light the main difference between the Latin and the Anglo-Saxon races, in the marked tendency of the one to submit to despotic government, and of the other to govern itself; of the one to stay at home under paternal authority, and of the other to leave the father's house and plunder the world for itself; of the sons of the one to accept wives given them, and of the other's children to marry as they please.

Roman family life, from Romulus to the year , was centred in the head of the house, whose position was altogether unassailable, whose requirements were necessities, and whose word was law. Next to him in place came the heir, who was brought up with a view to his exercising the same powers in his turn. After him, but far behind him in importance, if he promised to be strong, came the other sons, who, if they took wives at all, were expected to marry heiresses, and one of whom, almost as a matter of course, was brought up to be a churchman. The rest, if there were any, generally followed the career of arms, and remained unmarried; for heiresses of noble birth were few, and their guardians married them to eldest sons of great houses whenever possible, while the strength of caste prejudice made alliances of nobles with the daughters of rich plebeians extremely unusual.

It is possible to trace the daily life of a Roman family in the Middle Age from its regular routine of today, as out of what anyone may see in Italy the habits of the ancients can be reconstructed with more than approximate exactness. And yet it is out of the question to fix the period of the general transformation which ultimately turned the Rome of the Barons into the Rome of Napoleon's time, and converted the high-handed men of Sciarra Colonna's age into the effeminate fops of , when a gentleman of noble lineage, having received a box on the ear from another at high noon in the Corso, willingly followed the advice of his confessor, who counselled him to bear the affront with Christian meekness and present his other cheek to the smiter. Customs have remained, fashions have altogether changed; the outward forms of early living have survived, the spirit of life is quite another; and though some families still follow the patriarchal mode of existence, the patriarchs are gone, the law no longer lends itself to support household tyranny, and the subdivision of estates under the Napoleonic code is guiding an already existing democracy to the untried issue of a problematic socialism. Without attempting to establish a comparison upon the basis of a single cause, where so many are at work, it is permissible to note that while in England and Germany a more or less voluntary system of primogeniture is admitted and largely followed from choice, and while in the United States men230 are almost everywhere entirely free to dispose of their property as they please, and while the population and wealth of those countries are rapidly increasing, France, enforcing the division of estates among children, though she is accumulating riches, is faced by the terrible fact of a steadily diminishing census; and Italy, under the same laws, is not only rapidly approaching national bankruptcy, but is in parts already depopulated by an emigration so extensive that it can only be compared with the westward migration of the Aryan tribes. The forced subdivision of property from generation to generation is undeniably a socialistic measure, since it must, in the end, destroy both aristocracy and plutocracy; and it is surely a notable point that the two great European nations which have adopted it as a fundamental principle of good government should both be on the road to certain destruction, while those powers that have wholly and entirely rejected any such measure are filling the world with themselves and absorbing its wealth at an enormous and alarming rate.

VILLA BORGHESE VILLA BORGHESE

The art of the Renascence has left us splendid pictures of mediæval public life, which are naturally accepted as equally faithful representations of the life of every day. Princes and knights, in gorgeous robes and highly polished armour, ride on faultlessly caparisoned milk-white steeds; wondrous ladies wear not less wonderful gowns, fitted with a perfection which women seek in vain today, and embroidered with pearls and precious stones that might ransom a rajah; young pages, with glorious golden hair, stand ready at the elbows of their lords and ladies, or kneel in graceful attitude to deliver a letter, or stoop to bear a silken train, clad in garments which the modern costumer strives in vain to copy. After three or four centuries, the colours of those painted silks and satins are still richer than anything the loom can weave. In the great fresco, each individual of the multitude that fills a public place, or defiles in open procession under the noonday light, is not only a masterpiece of fashion, but a model of neatness; linen, delicate as woven gossamer, falls into folds as finely exact as an engraver's point could draw; velvet shoes tread without speck or spot upon the well-scoured pavement of a public street; men-at-arms grasp weapons and hold bridles with hands as carefully tended as any idle fine gentleman's, and there is neither fleck nor breath of dimness on the mirror-like steel of their armour; the very flowers, the roses and lilies that strew the way, are the perfection of fresh-cut hothouse blossoms; and when birds and beasts chance to be necessary to the composition of the picture, they are represented with no less care for a more than possible neatness, their coats are combed and curled, their attitudes are studied and graceful, they wear carefully made collars, ornamented with chased silver and gold.

Centuries have dimmed the wall-painting, sunshine232 has faded it, mould has mottled the broad surfaces of red and blue and green, and a later age has done away with the dresses represented; yet, when the frescos in the library of the Cathedral at Siena, for instance, were newly finished, they were the fashion-plates of the year and month, executed by a great artist, it is true, grouped with matchless skill and drawn with supreme mastery of art, but as far from representing the ordinary scenes of daily life as those terrible coloured prints published nowadays for tailors, in which a number of beautiful young gentlemen, in perfectly new clothes, lounge in stage attitudes on the one side, and an equal number of equally beautiful young butlers, coachmen, grooms and pages, in equally perfect liveries, appear to be discussing the æsthetics of an ideal and highly salaried service, at the other end of the same room. In the comparison there is all the brutal profanity of truth that shocks the reverence of romance; but in the respective relations of the great artist's masterpiece and of the poor modern lithograph to the realities of each period, there is the clue to the daily life of the Middle Age.

Living was outwardly rough as compared with the representations of it, though it was far more refined than in any other part of Europe, and Italy long set the fashion to the world in habits and manners. People kept their fine clothes for great occasions, there was a keeper of robes in every large household, and there233 were rooms set apart for the purpose. In every-day life, the Barons wore patched hose and leathern jerkins, stained and rusted by the joints of the armour that was so often buckled over them, or they went about their dwellings in long dressing-gowns which hid many shortcomings. When gowns, and hose, and jerkins were well worn, they were cut down for the boys of the family, and the fine dresses, only put on for great days, were preserved as heirlooms from generation to generation, whether they fitted the successive wearers or not. The beautiful tight-fitting hose which, in the paintings of the time, seem to fit like theatrical tights, were neither woven nor knitted, but were made of stout cloth, and must often have been baggy at the knees in spite of the most skilful cutting; and the party-coloured hose, having one leg of one piece of stuff and one of another, and sometimes each leg of two or more colours, were very likely first invented from motives of economy, to use up cuttings and leavings. Clothes were looked upon as permanent and very desirable property, and kings did not despise a gift of fine scarlet cloth, in the piece, to make them a gown or a cloak. As for linen, as late as the sixteenth century, the English thought the French nobles very extravagant because they put on a clean shirt once a fortnight and changed their ruffles once a week.

PALAZZO DI VENEZIA PALAZZO DI VENEZIA

The mediæval Roman nobles were most of them great farmers as well as fighters. Then, as now, land was the ultimate form of property, and its produce the usual form of wealth; and then, as now, many families were 'land-poor,' in the sense of owning tracts of country which yielded little or no income but represented considerable power, and furnished the owners with most of the necessaries of life, such rents as were collected being usually paid in kind, in oil and wine, in grain, fruit and vegetables, and even in salt meat, and horses, cattle for slaughtering and beasts of burden, not to speak of wool, hemp and flax, as well as firewood. But money was scarce and, consequently, all the things which only money could buy, so that a gown was a possession, and a corselet or a good sword a235 treasure. The small farmer of our times knows what it means to have plenty to eat and little to wear. His position is not essentially different from that of the average landed gentry in the Middle Age, not only in Italy, but all over Europe. In times when superiority lay in physical strength, courage, horsemanship and skill in the use of arms, the so-called gentleman was not distinguished from the plebeian by the newness or neatness of his clothes so much as by the nature and quality of the weapons he wore when he went abroad in peace or war, and very generally by being mounted on a good horse.

In his home he was simple, even primitive. He desired space more than comfort, and comfort more than luxury. His furniture consisted almost entirely of beds, chests and benches, with few tables except such as were needed for eating. Beds were supported by boards laid on trestles, raised very high above the floor to be beyond the reach of rats, mice and other creatures. The lower mattress was filled with the dried leaves of the maize, and the upper one contained wool, with which the pillows also were stuffed. The floors of dwelling rooms were generally either paved with bricks or made of a sort of cement, composed of lime, sand and crushed brick, the whole being beaten down with iron pounders, while in the moist state, during three days. There were no carpets, and fresh rushes were strewn everywhere on the floors, which in summer were236 first watered, like a garden path, to lay the dust. There was no glass in the windows of ordinary rooms, and the consequence was that during the daytime people lived almost in the open air, in winter as well as summer; sunshine was a necessity of existence, and sheltered courts and cloistered walks were built like reservoirs for the light and heat.

In the rooms, ark-shaped chests stood against the walls, to contain the ordinary clothes not kept in the general 'guardaroba.' In the deep embrasures of the windows there were stone seats, but there were few chairs, or none at all, in the bedrooms. At the head of each bed hung a rough little cross of dark wood —later, as carving became more general, a crucifix—and a bit of an olive branch preserved from Palm Sunday throughout the year. The walls themselves were scrupulously whitewashed; the ceilings were of heavy beams, supporting lighter cross-beams, on which in turn thick boards were laid to carry the cement floor of the room overhead.

Many hundred men-at-arms could be drawn up in the courtyards, and their horses stalled in the spacious stables. The kitchens, usually situated on the ground floor, were large enough to provide meals for half a thousand retainers, if necessary; and the cellars and underground prisons were a vast labyrinth of vaulted chambers, which not unfrequently communicated with the Tiber by secret passages. In restoring the palace237 of the Santacroce, a few years ago, a number of skeletons were discovered, some still wearing armour, and all most evidently the remains of men who had died violent deaths. One of them was found with a dagger driven through the skull and helmet. The hand that drove it must have been strong beyond the hands of common men.

The grand staircase led up from the sunny court to the state apartments, such as they were in those days. There, at least, there were sometimes carpets, luxuries of enormous value, and even before the Renascence the white walls were hung with tapestries, at least in part. In those times, too, there were large fireplaces in almost every room, for fuel was still plentiful in the Campagna and in the near mountains; and where the houses were practically open to the air all day, fires were an absolute necessity. Even in ancient times it is recorded that the Roman Senate, amidst the derisive jests of the plebeians, once had to adjourn on account of the extreme cold. People rose early in the Middle Age, dined at noon, slept in the afternoon when the weather was warm, and supped, as a rule, at 'one hour of the night,' that is to say an hour after 'Ave Maria,' which was rung half an hour after sunset, and was the end of the day of twenty-four hours. Noon was taken from the sun, but did not fall at a regular hour of the clock, and never fell at twelve. In winter, for instance, if the Ave Maria bell rang at half-past five of our modern time, the noon of the following day fell at 'half-past eighteen o'clock' by the mediæval clocks. In summer, it might fall as early as three quarters past fifteen; and this manner of reckoning time was common in Rome thirty-five years ago, and is not wholly unpractised in some parts of Italy still.

It was always an Italian habit, and a very healthy one, to get out of doors immediately on rising, and to put off making anything like a careful toilet till a much later hour. Breakfast, as we understand it, is an unknown meal in Italy, even now. Most people drink a cup of black coffee, standing; many eat a morsel of bread or biscuit with it and get out of doors as soon as they can; but the greediness of an Anglo-Saxon breakfast disgusts all Latins alike, and two set meals daily are thought to be enough for anyone, as indeed they are. The hard-working Italian hill peasant will sometimes toast himself a piece of corn bread before going to work, and eat it with a few drops of olive oil; and in the absence of tea or coffee, the people of the Middle Age often drank a mouthful of wine on rising to 'move the blood,' as they said. But that was all.

Every mediæval palace had its chapel, which was sometimes an adjacent church communicating with the house, and in many families it is even now the custom to hear the short low Mass at a very early hour. But probably nothing can give an adequate idea of the idleness of the Middle Age, when the day was once begun. Before the Renascence, there was no such thing as study, and there were hardly any pastimes except gambling and chess, both of which the girls and youths of the Decameron seem to have included in one contemptuous condemnation when they elected to spend their time in telling stories. The younger men of the household, of course, when not actually fighting, passed a certain number of hours in the practice of horsemanship and arms; but the only real excitement they knew was in love and war, the latter including everything between the battles of the Popes and Emperors, and the street brawls of private enemies, which generally drew blood and often ended in a death.

It does not appear that the idea of 'housekeeping' as the chief occupation of the Baron's wife ever entered into the Roman mind. In northern countries there has always been more equality between men and women, more respect for woman as an intelligent being, and less care for her as a valuable possession to be guarded against possible attacks from without. In Rome and the south of Italy the women in a great household were carefully separated from the men, and beyond the outer halls in which visitors were received, business transacted and politics discussed, there were closed doors, securely locked, leading 240 to the women's apartments beyond. In every Roman palace and fortress there was a revolving 'dumb-waiter' between the women's quarters and the men's, called the 'wheel,' and used as a means of communication. Through this the household supplies were daily handed in, for the cooking was very generally done by women, and through the same machine the prepared food was passed out to the men, the wheel being so arranged that men and women could not see each other, though they might hear each other speak. To all intents and purposes the system was oriental and the women were shut up in a harem. The use of the dumb-waiter survived the revolution in manners under the Renascence, and the wheel itself remains as a curiosity of past times in more than one Roman dwelling today. It had its uses and was not a piece of senseless tyranny. In order to keep up an armed force for all emergencies the Baron took under his protection as men-at-arms the most desperate ruffians, outlaws and outcasts whom he could collect, mostly men under sentence of banishment or death for highway robbery and murder, whose only chance of escaping torture and death lay in risking life and limb for a master strong enough to defy the law, the 'bargello' and the executioner, in his own house or castle, where such henchmen were lodged and fed, and were controlled by nothing but fear of the Baron himself, of his sons, when they were 241 grown up, and of his poorer kinsmen who lived with him. There were no crimes which such malefactors had not committed, or were not ready to commit for a word, or even for a jest. The women, on the other hand, were in the first place the ladies and daughters of the house, and of kinsmen, brought up in almost conventual solitude, when they were not actually educated in convents; and, secondly, young girls from the Baron's estates who served for a certain length of time, and were then generally married to respectable retainers. The position of twenty or thirty women and girls under the same roof with several hundreds of the most atrocious cutthroats of any age was undeniably such as to justify the most tyrannical measures for their protection.

There are traces, even now, of the enforced privacy in which they lived. For instance, no Roman lady of today will ever show herself at a window that looks on the street, except during Carnival, and in most houses something of the old arrangement of rooms is still preserved, whereby the men and women occupy different parts of the house.

One must try to call up the pictures of one day, to get any idea of those times; one must try and see the grey dawn stealing down the dark, unwindowed lower walls of the fortress that flanks the Church of the Holy Apostles,—the narrow and murky street below, the broad, dim space beyond, the mystery of the winding242 distances whence comes the first sound of the day, the far, high cry of the waterman driving his little donkey with its heavy load of water-casks. The beast stumbles along in the foul gloom, through the muddy ruts, over heaps of garbage at the corners, picking its way as best it can, till it starts with a snort and almost falls with its knees upon a dead man, whose thrice-stabbed body lies right across the way. The waterman, ragged, sandal-shod, stops, crosses himself, and drags his beast back hurriedly with a muttered exclamation of mingled horror, disgust and fear for himself, and makes for the nearest corner, stumbling along in his haste lest he should be found with the corpse and taken for the murderer. As the dawn forelightens, and the cries go up from the city, the black-hooded Brothers of Prayer and Death come in a little troop, their lantern still burning as they carry their empty stretcher, seeking for dead men; and they take up the poor nameless body and bear it away quickly from the sight of the coming day.

Then, as they disappear, the great bell of the Apostles' Church begins to toll the morning Angelus, half an hour before sunrise,—three strokes, then four, then five, then one, according to ancient custom, and then after a moment's silence, the swinging peal rings out, taken up and answered from end to end of the half-wasted city. A troop of men-at-arms ride up to the great closed gate 'in rusty armour marvellous ill-favoured,'243 as Shakespeare's stage direction has it, mud-splashed, their brown cloaks half concealing their dark and war-worn mail, their long swords hanging down and clanking against their huge stirrups, their beasts jaded and worn and filthy from the night raid in the Campagna, or the long gallop from Palestrina. The leader pounds three times at the iron-studded door with the hilt of his dagger, a sleepy porter, grey-bearded and cloaked, slowly swings back one half of the gate and the ruffians troop in, followed by the waterman who has gone round the fortress to avoid the dead body. The gate shuts again, with a long thundering rumble. High up, wooden shutters, behind which there is no glass, are thrown open upon the courtyard, and one window after another is opened to the morning air; on one side, girls and women look out, muffled in dark shawls; from the other grim, unwashed, bearded men call down to their companions, who have dismounted and are unsaddling their weary horses, and measuring out a little water to them, where water is a thing of price.

The leader goes up into the house to his master, to tell him of the night's doings, and while he speaks the Baron sits in a great wooden chair, in his long gown of heavy cloth, edged with coarse fox's fur, his feet in fur slippers, and a shabby cap upon his head, but a manly and stern figure, all the same, slowly munching a piece of toasted bread and sipping a few drops of old white wine from a battered silver cup.

Then Mass in the church, the Baron, his kinsmen, the ladies and the women kneeling in the high gallery above the altar, the men-at-arms and men-servants and retainers crouching below on the stone pavement; a dusky multitude, with a gleam of steel here and there, and red flashing eyes turned up with greedy longing towards the half-veiled faces of the women, met perhaps, now and then, by a furtive answering glance from under a veil or hoodlike shawl, for every woman's head is covered, but of the men only the old lord wears his cap, which he devoutly lifts at 'Gloria Patri' and 'Verbum Caro,' and at 'Sanctus' and at the consecration. It is soon over, and the day is begun, for the sun is fully risen and streams through the open unglazed windows as the maids sprinkle water on the brick floors, and sweep and strew fresh rushes, and roll back the mattresses on the trestle beds, which are not made again till evening. In the great courtyard, the men lead out the horses and mount them bareback and ride out in a troop, each with his sword by his side, to water them at the river, half a mile away, for not a single public fountain is left in Rome; and the grooms clean out the stables, while the peasants come in from the country, driving mules laden with provisions for the great household, and far away, behind barred doors, the women light the fires in the big kitchen.

Later again, the children of the noble house are taught to ride and fence in the open court; splendid boys with flowing hair, bright as gold or dark as night, dressed in rough hose and leathern jerkin, bright-eyed, fearless, masterful already in their play as a lion's whelps, watched from an upper window by their lady mother and their little sisters, and not soon tired of saddle or sword —familiar with the grooms and men by the great common instinct of fighting, but as far from vulgar as Polonius bade Laertes learn to be.

So morning warms to broad noon, and hunger makes it dinner-time, and the young kinsmen who have strolled abroad come home, one of them with his hand bound up in a white rag that has drops of blood on it, for he has picked a quarrel in the street and steel has been out, as usual, though no one has been killed, because the 'bargello' and his men were in sight, down there near the Orsini's theatre-fortress. And at dinner when the priest has blessed the table, the young men laugh about the scrimmage, while the Baron himself, who has killed a dozen men in battle, with his own hand, rebukes his sons and nephews with all the useless austerity which worn-out age wears in the face of unbroken youth. The meal is long, and they eat much, for there will be nothing more till night; they eat meat broth, thick with many vegetables and broken bread and lumps of boiled meat, and there246 are roasted meats and huge earthen bowls of salad, and there is cheese in great blocks, and vast quantities of bread, with wine in abundance, poured for each man by the butler into little earthen jugs from big earthenware flagons. They eat from trenchers of wood, well scoured with ashes; forks they have none, and most of the men use their own knives or daggers when they are not satisfied with the carving done for them by the carver. Each man, when he has picked a bone, throws it under the table to the house-dogs lying in wait on the floor, and from time to time a basin is passed and a little water poured upon the fingers. The Baron has a napkin of his own; there is one napkin for all the other men; the women generally eat by themselves in their own apartments, the so-called 'gentlemen' in the 'tinello,' and the men-at-arms and grooms, and all the rest, in the big lower halls near the kitchens, whence their food is passed out to them through the wheel.

After dinner, if it be summer and the weather hot, the gates are barred, the windows shut, and the whole household sleeps. Early or late, as the case may be, the lords and ladies and children take the air, guarded by scores of mounted men, riding towards that part of the city where they may neither meet their enemies nor catch a fever in the warm months. In rainy weather they pass the time as they can, with telling of many tales, short, dramatic and strong as the framework of a247 good play, with music, sometimes, and with songs, and with discussing of such news as there may be in such times. And at dusk the great bells ring to even-song, the oil lamp is swung up in the great staircase, the windows and gates are shut again, the torches and candles and little lamps are lit for supper, and at last, with rushlights, each finds the way along the ghostly corridors to bed and sleep. That was the day's round, and there was little to vary it in more peaceful times.

Over all life there was the hopeless, resentful dulness that oppressed men and women till it drove them half mad, to the doing of desperate things in love and war; there was the everlasting restraint of danger without and of forced idleness within—danger so constant that it ceased to be exciting and grew tiresome, idleness so oppressive that battle, murder and sudden death were a relief from the inactivity of sluggish peace; a state in which the mind was no longer a moving power in man, but only by turns the smelting pot and the anvil of half-smothered passions that now and then broke out with fire and flame and sword to slash and burn the world with a history of unimaginable horror.

That was the Middle Age in Italy. A poorer race would have gone down therein to a bloody destruction; but it was out of the Middle Age that the Italians were born again in the Renascence. It deserved the name.

REGION IV CAMPO MARZO

It was harvest time when the Romans at last freed themselves from the very name of Tarquin. In all the great field, between the Tiber and the City, the corn stood high and ripe, waiting for the sickle, while Brutus did justice upon his two sons, and upon the sons of his sister, and upon those 'very noble youths,' still the Tarquins' friends, who laid down their lives for their mistaken loyalty and friendship, and for whose devotion no historian has ever been brave enough, or generous enough, to say a word. It has been said that revolution is patriotism when it succeeds, treason when it fails, and in the converse, more than one brave man has died a traitor's death for keeping faith with a fallen king. Successful revolution denied those young royalists the charitable handful of earth and the four249 words of peace—'sit eis terra levis'—that should have laid their unquiet ghosts, and the brutal cynicism of history has handed down their names to the perpetual execration of mankind.

The corn stood high in the broad field which the Tarquins had taken from Mars and had ploughed and tilled for generations. The people went out and reaped the crop, and bound it in sheaves to be threshed for the public bread, but their new masters told them that it would be impious to eat what had been meant for kings, and they did as was commanded to them, meekly, and threw all into the river. Sheaf upon sheaf, load upon load, the yellow stream swept away the yellow ears and stalks, down to the shallows, where the whole mass stuck fast, and the seeds took root in the watery mud, and the stalks rotted in great heaps, and the island of the Tiber was first raised above the level of the water. Then the people burned the stubble and gave back the land to Mars, calling it the Campus Martius, after him.

There the young Romans learned the use of arms, and were taught to ride; and under sheds there stood those rows of wooden horses, upon which youths learned to vault, without step or stirrup, in their armour and sword in hand. There they ran foot-races in the clouds of dust whirled up from the dry ground, and threw the discus by the twisted thong as the young men of the hills do today, and the one who could250 reach the goal with the smallest number of throws was the winner,—there, under the summer sun and in the biting wind of winter, half naked, and tough as wolves, the boys of Rome laboured to grow up and be Roman men.

There, also, the great assemblies were held, the public meetings and the elections, when the people voted by passing into the wooden lists that were called 'Sheepfolds,' till Julius Cæsar planned the great marble portico for voting, and Agrippa finished it, making it nearly a mile round; and behind it, on the west side, a huge space was kept open for centuries, called the Villa Publica, where the censors numbered the people. The ancient Campus took in a wide extent of land, for it included everything outside the Servian wall, from the Colline Gate to the river. All that visibly bears its name today is a narrow street that runs southward from the western end of San Lorenzo in Lucina. The Region of Campo Marzo, however, is still one of the largest in the city, including all that lies within the walls from Porta Pinciana, by Capo le Case, Via Frattina, Via di Campo Marzo and Via della Stelletta, past the Church of the Portuguese and the Palazzo Moroni,—known by Hawthorne's novel as 'Hilda's Tower,'—and thence to the banks of the Tiber.

PIAZZA DI SPAGNA PIAZZA DI SPAGNA

From the Renascence until the recent extension of the city on the south and southeast, this Region was the more modern part of Rome. In the Middle Age it was held by the Colonna, who had fortified the tomb of Augustus and one or two other ruins. Later it became the strangers' quarter. The Lombards established themselves near the Church of Saint Charles, in the Corso; the English, near Saint Ives, the little church with the strange spiral tower, built against the University of the Sapienza; the Greeks lived in the Via de' Greci; the Burgundians in the Via Borgognona, and thence to San Claudio, where they had their Hospice; and so on, almost every nationality being established in a colony of its own; and the English visitors of today are still inclined to252 think the Piazza di Spagna the most central point of Rome, whereas to Romans it seems to be very much out of the way.

The tomb of Augustus, which served as the model for the greater Mausoleum of Hadrian, dominated the Campus Martius, and its main walls are still standing, though hidden by many modern houses. The tomb of the Julian Cæsars rose on white marble foundations, a series of concentric terraces, planted with cypress trees, to the great bronze statue of Augustus that crowned the summit. Here rested the ashes of Augustus, of the young Marcellus, of Livia, of Tiberius, of Caligula, and of many others whose bodies were burned in the family Ustrinum near the tomb itself. Plundered by Alaric, and finally ruined by Robert Guiscard, when he burnt the city, it became a fortress under the Colonna, and is included, with the fortress of Monte Citorio, in a transfer of property made by one member of the family to another in the year . Ruined at last, it became a bull ring in the last century and in the beginning of this one, when Leo the Twelfth forbade bull-fighting. Then it was a theatre, the scene of Salvini's early triumphs. Today it is a circus, dignified by the name of the reigning sovereign.

Few people know that bull-fights were common in Rome eighty years ago. The indefatigable Baracconi once talked with the son of the last bull-fighter. So far as one may judge, it appears that during the Middle253 Age, and much later, it was the practice of butchers to bait animals in their own yards, before slaughtering them, in the belief that the cruel treatment made the meat more tender, and they admitted the people to see the sport. From this to a regular arena was but a step, and no more suitable place than the tomb of the Cæsars could be found for the purpose. A regular manager took possession of it, provided the victims, both bulls and Roman buffaloes, and hired the fighters. It does not appear that the beasts were killed during the entertainment, and one of the principal attractions was the riding of the maddened bull three times round the circus; savage dogs were also introduced, but in all other respects the affair was much like a Spanish bull-fight, and quite as popular; when the chosen bulls were led in from the Campagna, the Roman princes used to ride far out to meet them with long files of mounted servants in gala liveries, coming back at night in torchlight procession. And again, after the fight was over, the circus was illuminated, and there was a small display of Bengal lights, while the fashionable world of Rome met and gossiped away the evening in the arena, happily thoughtless and forgetful of all the spot had been and had meant in history.

The new Rome sinks out of sight below the level of the old, as one climbs the heights of the Janiculum on the west of the city, or the gardens of the Pincio on the east. The old monuments and the old churches254 still rise above the dreary wastes of modern streets, and from the spot whence Messalina looked down upon the cypresses of the first Emperor's mausoleum, the traveller of today descries the cheap metallic roof which makes a circus of the ancient tomb.

For it was in the gardens of Lucullus that Mark Antony's great-grandchild felt the tribune's sword in her throat, and in the neat drives and walks of the Pincio, where pretty women in smart carriages laugh over today's gossip and tomorrow's fashion, and the immaculate dandy idles away an hour and a cigarette, the memory of Messalina calls up a tragedy of shades. Less than thirty years after Augustus had breathed out his old age in peace, Rome was ruled again by terror and blood, and the triumph of a woman's sins was the beginning of the end of the Julian race. The great historian who writes of her guesses that posterity may call the truth a fable, and tells the tale so tersely and soberly from first to last, that the strength of his words suggests a whole mystery of evil. Without Tiberius, there could have been no Messalina, nor, without her, could Nero have been possible; and the worst of the three is the woman—the archpriestess of all conceivable crime. Tacitus gives Tiberius one redeeming touch. Often the old Emperor came almost to Rome, even to the gardens by the Tiber, and then turned back to the rocks of Capri and the solitude of the sea, in mortal shame of his monstrous deeds, as if not daring255 to show himself in the city. With Nero, the measure was full, and the world rose and destroyed him. Messalina knew no shame, and the Romans submitted to her, and but for a court intrigue and a frightened favourite she might have lived out her life unhurt. In the eyes of the historian and of the people of her time her greatest misdeed was that while her husband Claudius, the Emperor, was alive she publicly celebrated her marriage with the handsome Silius, using all outward legal forms. Our modern laws of divorce have so far accustomed our minds to such deeds that, although we miss the legal formalities which would necessarily precede such an act in our time, we secretly wonder at the effect it produced upon the men of that day, and are inclined to smile at the epithets of 'impious' and 'sacrilegious' which it called down upon Messalina, whose many other frightful crimes had elicited much more moderate condemnation. Claudius, himself no novice or beginner in horrors, hesitated long after he knew the truth, and it was the favourite Narcissus who took upon himself to order the Empress' death. Euodus, his freedman, and a tribune of the guard were sent to make an end of her. Swiftly they went up to the gardens—the gardens of the Pincian—and there they found her, beautiful, dark, dishevelled, stretched upon the marble floor, her mother Lepida crouching beside her, her mother, who in the bloom of her daughter's evil life had turned from her, but in her extreme need was overcome with pity. There knelt Domitia Lepida, urging the terror-mad woman not to wait the executioner, since life was over and nothing remained but to lend death the dignity of suicide. But the dishonoured self was empty of courage, and long-drawn weeping choked her useless lamentations. Then suddenly the doors were flung open with a crash, and the stern tribune stood silent in the hall, while the freedman Euodus screamed out curses, after the way of triumphant slaves. From her mother's hand the lost Empress took the knife at last and trembling laid it to her breast and throat, with weakly frantic fingers that could not hurt herself; the silent tribune killed her with one straight thrust, and when they brought the news to Claudius sitting at supper, and told him that Messalina had perished, his face did not change, and he said nothing as he held out his cup to be filled.

PIAZZA DEL POPOLO PIAZZA DEL POPOLO

She died somewhere on the Pincian hill. Romance would choose the spot exactly where the nunnery of the Sacred Heart stands, at the Trinità de' Monti, looking down De Sanctis' imposing 'Spanish' steps; and the house in which the noble girls of modern Rome are sent to school may have risen upon the foundations of Messalina's last abode. Or it may be that the place was further west, in the high grounds of the French Academy, or on the site of the academy itself, at the gates of the public garden, just where the old stone fountain bubbles and murmurs under the shade of the thick ilex trees. Most of that land once belonged to Lucullus, the conqueror of Mithridates, the

Academic philosopher, the arch feaster, and the man who first brought cherries to Italy.

TRINITÀ DE' MONTI TRINITÀ DE' MONTI

The last descendant of Julia, the last sterile monster of the Julian race, Nero, was buried at the foot of the same hill. Alive, he was condemned by the Senate to be beaten to death in the Comitium; dead by his own hand, he received imperial honours, and his ashes rested for a thousand years where they had been laid by his two old nurses and a woman who had loved him. And during ten centuries the people believed that his terrible ghost haunted the hill, attended and served by thousands of demon crows that rested in the branches of the trees about his tomb, and flew forth to do evil at his bidding, till at last Pope Paschal the Second cut down with his own hands the walnut trees which crowned the summit, and commanded that the mausoleum should be destroyed, and the ashes of Nero scattered to the winds, that he might build a parish church on the spot and dedicate it to Saint Mary. It is said, too, that the Romans took the marble urn in which the ashes had been, and used it as a public measure for salt in the old market-place of the Capitol. A number of the rich Romans of the Renascence afterwards contributed money to the restoration of the church and built themselves chapels within it, as tombs for their descendants, so that it is the burial-place of many of those wealthy families that settled in Rome and took possession of the Corso when the Barons still held the less central parts of the city with their mediæval fortresses. Sixtus the Fourth and Julius the Second are buried in Saint Peter's, but their chapel was here, and here lie others of the della Rovere race, and many of the Chigi and Pallavicini and Theodoli; and here, in strange coincidence, Alexander the Sixth, the worst of the Popes, erected a high altar on the very spot where the worst of the Emperors had been buried. It is gone now, but the strange fact is not forgotten.

Far across the beautiful square, at the entrance to the Corso, twin churches seem to guard the way like sentinels, built, it is said, to replace two chapels which once stood at the head of the bridge of Sant' Angelo; demolished because, when Rome was sacked by the Constable of Bourbon, they had been held as important points by the Spanish soldiers in besieging the Castle, and it was not thought wise to leave such useful outworks for any possible enemy in the future. Alexander the Seventh, the Chigi Pope, died, and left the work unfinished; and a folk story tells how a poor old woman who lived near by saved what she could for many years, and, dying, left one hundred and fifty scudi to help the completion of the buildings; and Cardinal Gastaldi, who had been refused the privilege of placing his arms upon a church which he had desired to build in Bologna, and was looking about for an opportunity of perpetuating his name, finished the two churches, his attention having been first called to them by the old woman's humble bequest.

As for the Pincio itself, and the ascent to it from the Piazza del Popolo, all that land was but a grass-grown hillside, crowned by a few small and scattered villas and scantily furnished with trees, until the beginning of the present century; and the public gardens of the earlier time were those of the famous and beautiful Villa Medici, which Napoleon the First bestowed upon the French Academy. It was there that the fashionable260 Romans of the seventeenth and eighteenth centuries used to meet, and walk, and be carried about in gilded sedan-chairs, and flirt, and gossip, and exchange views on politics and opinions about the latest scandal. That was indeed a very strange society, further from us in many ways than the world of the Renascence, or even of the Crusades; for the Middle Age was strong in the sincerity of its beliefs, as we are powerful in the cynicism of our single-hearted faith in riches; but the fabric of the seventeenth and eighteenth centuries was founded upon the abuse of an already declining power; it was built up in the most extraordinary and elaborate affectation, and it was guarded by a system of dissimulation which outdid that of our own day by many degrees, and possibly surpassed the hypocrisy of any preceding age.

No one, indeed, can successfully uphold the idea that the high development of art in any shape is of necessity coincident with a strong growth of religion or moral conviction. Perugino made no secret of being an atheist; Lionardo da Vinci was a scientific sceptic; Raphael was an amiable rake, no better and no worse than the majority of those gifted pupils to whom he was at once a model of perfection and an example of free living; and those who maintain that art is always the expression of a people's religion have but an imperfect acquaintance with the age of Praxiteles, Apelles and Zeuxis. Yet the idea itself has a foundation, lying in something261 which is as hard to define as it is impossible to ignore; for if art be not a growth out of faith, it is always the result of a faith that has been, since although it is possible to conceive of religion without art, it is out of the question to think of art as a whole, without a religious origin; and as the majority of writers find it easier to describe scenes and emotions, when a certain lapse of time has given them what painters call atmospheric perspective, so the Renascence began when memory already clothed the ferocious realism of mediæval Christianity in the softer tones of gentle chivalry and tender romance. It is often said, half in jest, that, in order to have intellectual culture, a man must at least have forgotten Latin, if he cannot remember it, because the fact of having learned it leaves something behind that cannot be acquired in any other way. Similarly, I think that art of all sorts has reached its highest level in successive ages when it has aimed at recalling, by an illusion, a once vivid reality from a not too distant past. And so when it gives itself up to the realism of the present, it impresses the senses rather than the thoughts, and misses its object, which is to bring within our mental reach what is beyond our physical grasp; and when, on the other hand, it goes back too far, it fails in execution, because its models are not only out of sight, but out of mind, and it cannot touch us because we can no longer feel even a romantic interest in the real or imaginary events which it attempts to describe.

The subject is too high to be lightly touched, and too wide to be touched more than lightly here; but in this view of it may perhaps be found some explanation of the miserable poverty of Italian art in the eighteenth century, foreshadowed by the decadence of the seventeenth, which again is traceable to the dissipation of force and the disappearance of individuality that followed the Renascence, as inevitably as old age follows youth. Besides all necessary gifts of genius, the development of art seems to require that a race should not only have leisure for remembering, but should also have something to remember which may be worthy of being recalled and perhaps of being imitated. Progress may be the road to wealth and health, and to such happiness as may be derived from both; but the advance of civilization is the path of thought, and its landmarks are not inventions nor discoveries, but those very great creations of the mind which ennoble the heart in all ages; and as the idea of progress is inseparable from that of growing riches, so is the true conception of civilization indivisible from thoughts of beauty and nobility. In the seventeenth and eighteenth centuries, Italy had almost altogether lost sight of these; art was execrable, fashion was hideous, morality meant hypocrisy; the surest way to power lay in the most despicable sort of intrigue, and inward and spiritual faith was as rare as outward and visible devoutness was general.

That was the society which frequented the Villa263 Medici on fine afternoons, and it is hard to see wherein its charm lay, if, indeed, it had any. Instead of originality, its conversation teemed with artificial conventionalisms; instead of nature, it exhibited itself in the disguise of fashions more inconvenient, uncomfortable and ridiculous than those of any previous or later times; it delighted in the impossibly nonsensical 'pastoral' verses which we find too silly to read; and in place of wit, it clothed gross and cruel sayings in a thin remnant of worn-out classicism. It had not the frankly wicked recklessness of the French aristocracy between Lewis the Fourteenth and the Revolution, nor the changing contrasts of brutality, genius, affectation and Puritanical austerity which marked England's ascent, from the death of Edward the Sixth to the victories of Nelson and Wellington; still less had it any of those real motives for existence which carried Germany through her long struggle for life. It had little which we are accustomed to respect in men and women, and yet it had something which we lack today, and which we unconsciously envy—it had a colour of its own. Wandering under the ancient ilexes of those sad and beautiful gardens, meeting here and there a few silent and soberly clad strangers, one cannot but long for the brilliancy of two centuries ago, when the walks were gay with brilliant dresses, and gilded chairs, and servants in liveries of scarlet and green and gold, and noble ladies, tottering a few steps on their ridiculous264 high heels, and men bewigged and becurled, their useless little hats under their arms, and their embroidered coat tails flapping against their padded, silk-stockinged calves; and red-legged, unpriestly Cardinals who were not priests even in name, but only the lay life-peers of the Church; and grave Bishops with their secretaries; and laughing abbés, whose clerical dress was the accustomed uniform of government office, which they still wore when they were married, and were fathers of families. There is little besides colour to recommend the picture, but at least there is that.

The Pincian hill has always been the favourite home of artists of all kinds, and many lived at one time or another in the little villas that once stood there, and in the houses in the Via Sistina and southward, and up towards the Porta Pinciana. Guido Reni, the Caracci, Salvator Rosa, Poussin, Claude Lorrain, have all left the place the association of their presence, and the Zuccheri brothers built themselves the house which still bears their name, just below the one at the corner of the Trinità de' Monti, known to all foreigners as the 'Tempietto' or little temple. But the Villa Medici stands as it did long ago, its walls uninjured, its trees grander than ever, its walks unchanged. Soft-hearted Baracconi, in love with those times more than with the Middle Age, speaks half tenderly of the people who used to meet there, calling them collectively a gay and light-hearted society, gentle, idle, full of graceful265 thoughts and delicate perceptions, brilliant reflections and light charms; he regrets the gilded chairs, the huge built-up wigs, the small sword of the 'cavalier servente,' and the abbé's silk mantle, the semi-platonic friendships, the jests borrowed from Goldoni, the 'pastoral' scandal, and exchange of compliments and madrigals and epigrams, and all the brilliant powdered train of that extinct world.

VILLA MEDICI VILLA MEDICI

Whatever life may have been in those times, that world died in a pretty tableau, after the manner of Watteau's paintings; it meant little and accomplished little, and though its bright colouring brings it for a moment to the foreground, it has really not much to do with the Rome we know nor with the Rome one thinks of in266 the past, always great, always sad, always tragic, as no other city in the world can ever be.

Ignorance, tradition, imagination, romance,—call it what you will,—has chosen the long-closed Pincian Gate for the last station of blind Belisarius. There, says the tale, the ancient conqueror, the banisher and maker of Popes, the favourite and the instrument of imperial Theodora, stood begging his bread at the gate of the city he had won and lost, leaning upon the arm of the fair girl child who would not leave him, and stretching forth his hand to those that passed by, with a feeble prayer for alms, pathetic as Œdipus in the utter ruin of his life and fortune. A truer story tells how Pope Silverius, humble and gentle, and hated by Theodora, went up to the Pincian villa to answer the accusation of conspiring with the Goths, when he himself had opened the gates of Rome to Belisarius; and how he was led into the great hall where the warrior's wife, Theodora's friend, the beautiful and evil Antonina, lay with half-closed eyes upon her splendid couch, while Belisarius sat beside her feet, toying with her jewels. There the husband and wife accused the Pope, and judged him without hearing, and condemned him without right; and they caused him to be stripped of his robes, and clad as a poor monk and driven out to far exile, that they might set up the Empress Theodora's Pope in his place; and with him they drove out many Roman nobles.

And it is said that when Silverius was dead of a267 broken heart in the little island of Palmaria, Belisarius repented of his deeds and built the small Church of Santa Maria de' Crociferi, behind the fountain of Trevi, in partial expiation of his fault, and there, to prove the truth of the story, the tablet that tells of his repentance has stood nearly fourteen hundred years and may be read today, on the east wall, towards the Via de' Poli. The man who conquered Africa for Justinian, seized Sicily, took Rome, defended it successfully against the Goths, reduced Ravenna, took Rome from the Goths again, and finally rescued Constantinople, was disgraced more than once; but he was not blinded, nor did he die in exile or in prison, for at the end he breathed his last in the enjoyment of his freedom and his honours; and the story of his blindness is the fabrication of an ignorant Greek monk who lived six hundred years later and confounded Justinian's great general with the romantic and unhappy John of Cappadocia, who lived at the same time, was a general at the same time, and incurred the displeasure of that same pious, proud, avaricious Theodora, actress, penitent and Empress, whose paramount beauty held the Emperor in thrall for life, and whose surpassing cruelty imprinted an indelible seal of horror upon his glorious reign—of her who, when she delivered a man to death, admonished the executioner with an oath, saying, 'By Him who liveth for ever, if thou failest, I will cause thee to be flayed alive.'268

Another figure rises at the window of the Tuscan Ambassador's great villa, with the face of a man concerning whom legend has also found much to invent and little to say that is true, a man of whom modern science has rightly made a hero, but whom prejudice and ignorance have wrongly crowned as a martyr—

Galileo Galilei. Tradition represents him as languishing, laden with chains, in the more or less mythical prisons of the Inquisition; history tells very plainly that his first confinement consisted in being the honoured guest of the Tuscan Ambassador in the latter's splendid residence in Rome, and that his last imprisonment was a relegation to the beautiful castle of the Piccolomini near Siena, than which the heart of man could hardly desire a more lovely home. History affirms beyond doubt, moreover, that Galileo was the personal friend of that learned and not illiberal Barberini, Pope Urban the Eighth, under whose long reign the Copernican system was put on trial, who believed in that system as Galileo did, who read his books and talked with him; and who, when the stupid technicalities of the ecclesiastic courts declared the laws of the universe to be nonsense, gave his voice against the decision, though he could not officially annul it without scandal. 'It was not my intention,' said the Pope in the presence of witnesses, 'to condemn Galileo. If the matter had depended upon me, the decree of the Index which condemned his doctrines should never have been pronounced.'269

That Galileo's life was saddened by the result of the absurd trial, and that he was nominally a prisoner for a long time, is not to be denied. But that he suffered the indignities and torments recorded in legend is no more true than that Belisarius begged his bread at the Porta Pinciana. He lived in comfort and in honour with the Ambassador in the Villa Medici, and many a time from those lofty windows, unchanged since before his day, he must have watched the earth turning with him from the sun at evening, and meditated upon the emptiness of the ancient phrase that makes the sun 'set' when the day is done —thinking of the world, perhaps, as turning upon its other side, with tired eyes, and ready for rest and darkness and refreshment, after long toil and heat.

One may stand under those old trees before the Villa Medici, beside the ancient fountain facing Saint Peter's distant dome, and dream the great review of history, and call up a vast, changing picture at one's feet between the heights and the yellow river. First, the broad corn-field of the Tarquin Kings, rich and ripe under the evening breeze of summer that runs along swiftly, bending the golden surface in soft moving waves from the Tiber's edge to the foot of the wooded slope. Then, the hurried harvesting, the sheaves cast into the river, the dry, stiff stubble baking in the sun, and presently the men of Rome coming270 forth in procession from the dark Servian wall on the left to dedicate the field to the War God with prayer and chant and smoking sacrifice. By and by the stubble trodden down under horses' hoofs, the dusty plain the exercising ground of young conquerors, the voting place, later, of a strong Republic, whither the centuries went out to choose their consuls, to decide upon peace or war, to declare the voice of the people in grave matters, while the great signal flag waved on the Janiculum, well in sight though far away, to fall suddenly at the approach of any foe and suspend the 'comitia' on the instant. And in the flat and dusty plain, buildings begin to rise; first, the Altar of Mars and the holy place of the infernal gods, Dis and Proserpine; later, the great 'Sheepfold,' the lists and hustings for the voting, and, encroaching a little upon the training ground, the temple of Venus Victorious and the huge theatre of Pompey, wherein the Orsini held their own so long; but in the times of Lucullus, when his gardens and his marvellous villa covered the Pincian hill, the plain was still a wide field, and still the field of Mars, without the walls, broken by few landmarks, and trodden to deep white dust by the scampering hoofs of half-drilled cavalry. Under the Emperors, then, first beautified in part, as Cæsar traces the great Septa for the voting, and Augustus erects the Altar of Peace and builds up his cypress-clad tomb, crowned by his own image, and Agrippa raises his triple temple, and Hadrian builds the Pantheon upon its ruins, while the obelisk that now stands on Monte Citorio before the House of Parliament points out the brass-figured hours on the broad marble floor of the first Emperor's sun-clock and marks the high noon of Rome's glory—and the Portico of Neptune and many other splendid works spring up. Isis and Serapis have a temple next, and Domitian's race-course appears behind Agrippa's Baths, straight and white. By and by the Antonines raise columns and triumphal arches, but always to southward, leaving the field of Mars a field still, for its old uses, and the tired recruits, sweating from exercise, gather under the high shade of Augustus' tomb at midday for an hour's rest.

Last of all, the great temple of the Sun, with its vast portico, and the Mithræum at the other end, and when the walls of Aurelian are built, and when ruin comes upon Rome from the north, the Campus Martius is still almost an open stretch of dusty earth on which soldiers have learned their trade through a thousand years of hard training.

Not till the poor days when the waterless, ruined city sends its people down from the heights to drink of the muddy stream does Campo Marzo become a town, and then, around the castle-tomb of the Colonna and the castle-theatre of the Orsini the wretched houses begin to rise here and there, thickening to a low, dark forest of miserable dwellings threaded through and through, up and down and crosswise, by narrow and crooked streets, out of which by degrees the lofty churches and palaces of the later age are to spring up. From a training ground it has become a fighting ground, a labyrinth of often barricaded ways and lanes, deeper and darker towards the water-gates cut in the wall that runs along the Tiber, from Porta del Popolo nearly to the island of Saint Bartholomew, and almost all that is left of Rome is crowded and huddled into the narrow pen overshadowed and dominated here and there by black fortresses and brown brick towers. The man who then might have looked down from the Pincian hill would have seen that sight; houses little better than those of the poorest mountain village in the Southern Italy of today, black with smoke, black with dirt, blacker with patches made by shadowy windows that had no glass. A silent town, too, surly and defensive; now and then the call of the water-carrier disturbs the stillness, more rarely, the cry of a wandering peddler; and sometimes a distant sound of hoofs, a far clash of iron and steel, and the echoing yell of furious fighting men—'Orsini!' 'Colonna!'—the long-drawn syllables coming up distinct through the evening air to the garden where Messalina died, while the sun sets red behind the spire of old Saint Peter's across the river, and gilds the huge girth of dark Sant' Angelo to a rusty red, like battered iron bathed in blood.

Back come the Popes from Avignon, and streets grow wider and houses cleaner and men richer—all for the Bourbon's Spaniards to sack, and burn, and destroy before the last city grows up, and the rounded domes raise their helmet-like heads out of the chaos, and the broad Piazza del Popolo is cleared, and old Saint Peter's goes down in dust to make way for the Cathedral of all Christendom as it stands. Then far away, on Saint Peter's evening, when it is dusk, the great dome, and the small domes, and the colonnades, and the broad façade are traced in silver lights that shine out quietly as the air darkens. The solemn bells toll the first hour of the June night; the city is hushed, and all at once the silver lines are turned to gold, as the red flame runs in magic change from the topmost cross down the dome, in rivers, to the roof, and the pillars and the columns of the square below—the grandest illumination of the grandest church the world has ever seen.

REGION V PONTE

The Region of Ponte, 'the Bridge,' takes its name from the ancient Triumphal Bridge which led from the city to the Vatican Fields, and at low water some fragments of the original piers may be seen in the river at the bend just below Ponte Sant' Angelo, between the Church of Saint John of the Florentines on the one bank, and the Hospital of Santo Spirito on the other. In the Middle Age, according to Baracconi and others, the broken arches still extended into the stream, and upon them was built a small fortress, the outpost of the Orsini on that side. The device, however, appears to represent a portion of the later Bridge of Sant' Angelo, built upon the foundations of the Ælian Bridge of 275 Hadrian, which connected his tomb with the Campus Martius. The Region consists of the northwest point of the city, bounded by the Tiber, from Monte Brianzo round the bend, and down stream to the new Lungara bridge, and on the land side by a very irregular line running across the Corso Vittorio Emanuele, close to the Chiesa Nuova, and then eastward and northward in a zigzag, so as to take in most of the fortresses of the Orsini family, Monte

Giordano, Tor Millina, Tor Sanguigna, and the now demolished Torre di Nona. The Sixth and Seventh Regions adjacent to the Fifth and to each other would have to be included in order to take in all that part of Rome once held by the only family that rivalled, and sometimes surpassed, the Colonna in power.

As has been said before, the original difference between the two was that the Colonna were Ghibellines and for the Emperors, while the Orsini were Guelphs and generally adhered to the Popes. In the violent changes of the Middle Age, it happened indeed that the Colonna had at least one Pope of their own, and that more than one, such as Nicholas the Fourth, favoured their race to the point of exciting popular indignation. But, on the whole, they kept to their parties. When Lewis the Bavarian was to be crowned by force, Sciarra Colonna crowned him; when Henry the Seventh of Luxemburg had come to Rome for the same purpose, a few years earlier, the Orsini[276] had been obliged to be satisfied with a sort of second-rate coronation at Saint John Lateran's; and when the struggle between the two families was at its height, nearly two centuries later, and Sixtus the Fourth 'assumed the part of mediator,' as the chronicle expresses it, one of his first acts of mediation was to cut off the head of a Colonna, and his next was to lay regular siege to the strongholds of the family in the Roman hills; but before he had brought this singular process of mediation to an issue he suddenly died, the Colonna returned to their dwellings in Rome 'with great clamour and triumph,' got the better of the Orsini, and proceeded to elect a Pope after their own hearts, in the person of Cardinal Cibo, of Genoa, known as Innocent the Eighth. He it is who lies under the beautiful bronze monument in the inner left aisle of Saint Peter's, which shows him holding in his hand a model of the spear-head that pierced Christ's side, a relic believed to have been sent to the Pope as a gift by Sultan Bajazet the Second.

The origin of the hatred between Colonna and Orsini is unknown, for the archives of the former have as yet thrown no light upon the subject, and those of the latter were almost entirely destroyed by fire in the last century. In the year , Pope Clement the Fifth was elected Pope at Perugia. He was a Frenchman, and was Archbishop of Bordeaux, the candidate of Philip the Fair, whose tutor had been a Colonna, and he was[277] chosen by the opposing factions of two Orsini cardinals because the people of Perugia were tired of a quarrel that had lasted eleven months, and had adopted the practical and always infallible expedient of deliberately starving the conclave to a vote. Muratori calls it a scandalous and illicit election, which brought about the ruin of Italy and struck a memorable blow at the power of the Holy See. Though not a great man, Philip the Fair was one of the cleverest that ever lived. Before the election he had made his bishop swear upon the Sacred Host to accept his conditions, without expressing them all; and the most important proved to be the transference of the Papal See to France. The new Pope obeyed his master, established himself in Avignon, and the King to all intents and purposes had taken the Pontificate captive and lost no time in using it for his own ends against the Empire, his hereditary foe. Such, in a few words, is the history of that memorable transaction; and but for the previous quarrels of Colonna, Caetani and Orsini, it could never have taken place. The Orsini repented bitterly of what they had done, for one of Clement the Fifth's first acts was to 'annul altogether all sentences whatsoever pronounced against the Colonna.'

But the Pope being gone, the Barons had Rome in their power and used it for a battlefield. Four years later, we find in Villani the first record of a skirmish fought between Orsini and Colonna. In the month of October, , says the chronicler, certain of the Orsini and of the Colonna met outside the walls of Rome with their followers, to the number of four hundred horse, and fought together, and the Colonna won; and there died the Count of Anguillara, and six of the Orsini were taken, and Messer Riccardo degli Annibaleschi who was in their company.

Three years afterwards, Henry of Luxemburg alternately feasted and fought his way to Rome to be crowned Emperor in spite of Philip the Fair, the Tuscan league and Robert, King of Naples, who sent a thousand horsemen out of the south to hinder the coronation. In a day Rome was divided into two great camps. Colonna held for the Emperor the Lateran, Santa Maria Maggiore, the Colosseum, the Torre delle Milizie,—the brick tower on the lower part of the modern Via Nazionale,—the Pantheon, as an advanced post in one direction, and Santa Sabina, a church that was almost a fortress, on the south, by the Tiber,—a chain of fortresses which would be formidable in any modern revolution. Against Henry, however, the Orsini held the Vatican and Saint Peter's, the Castle of Sant' Angelo and all Trastevere, their fortresses in the Region of Ponte, and, moreover, the Capitol itself. The parties were well matched, for, though Henry entered Rome on the seventh of May, the struggle lasted till the twenty-ninth of June.

Those who have seen revolutions can guess at the desperate fighting in the barricaded streets, and at the well-guarded bridges from one end of the city to the other. Backwards and forwards the battle raged for days and weeks, by day and night, with small time for rest and refreshment. Forward rode the Colonna, the stolid Germans, Henry himself, the eagle of the Empire waving in the dim streets beside the flag that displayed the simple column in a plain field. It is not hard to hear and see it all again—the clanging gallop of armoured knights, princes, nobles and bishops, with visors down, and long swords and maces in their hands, the high, fierce cries of the light-armed footmen, the bowmen and the slingers, the roar of the rabble rout behind, the shrill voices of women at upper windows, peering down for the face of brother, husband, or lover in the dashing press below,—the dust, the heat, the fierce June sunshine blazing on broad steel, and the deep, black shadows putting out all light as the bands rush past. Then, on a sudden, the answering shout of the Orsini, the standard of the Bear, the Bourbon lilies of Anjou, the scarlet and white colours of the Guelph house, the great black horses, and the dark mail—the enemies surging together in the street like swift rivers of loose iron meeting in a stone channel, with a rending crash and the quick hammering of steel raining desperate blows on steel—horses rearing their height, footmen crushed, knights reeling in the saddle, sparks flying, steel-clad arms and long280 swords whirling in great circles through the air. Foremost of all in fight the Bishop of Liège, his purple mantle flying back from his corselet, trampling down everything, sworn to win the barricade or die, riding at it like a madman, forcing his horse up to it over the heaps of quivering bodies that made a causeway, leaping it alone at last, like a demon in air, and standing in the thick of the Orsini, slaying to right and left.

In an instant they had him down and bound and prisoner, one man against a thousand; and they fastened him behind a man-at-arms, on the crupper, to take him into Sant' Angelo alive. But a soldier, whose brother he had slain a moment earlier, followed stealthily on foot and sought the joint in the back of the armour, and ran in his pike quickly, and killed him—'whereof,' says the chronicle, 'was great pity, for the Bishop was a man of high courage and authority.' But on the other side of the barricade, those who had followed him so far, and lost him, felt their hearts sink, for not one of them could do what he had done; and after that, though they fought a whole month longer, they had but little hope of ever getting to the Vatican. So the Colonna took Henry up to the Lateran, where they were masters, and he was crowned there by three cardinals in the Pope's stead, while the Orsini remained grimly intrenched in their own quarter, and each party held its own, even after Henry had prudently retired to Tivoli, in the hills.

ISLAND IN THE TIBER ISLAND IN THE TIBER

At last the great houses made a truce and a compromise, by which they attempted to govern Rome jointly, and chose Sciarra—the same who had taken Pope Boniface prisoner in Anagni—and Matteo Orsini of Monte Giordano, to be Senators together; and there was peace between them for a time, in the year in which Rienzi was born. But in that very year, as though foreshadowing his destiny, the rabble of Rome rose up, and chose a dictator; and somehow, by surprise or treachery, he got possession of the Barons' chief fortresses, and of Sant' Angelo, and set up the standard of terror against the nobles. In a few days he sacked and burned their strongholds, and the high and mighty lords who had made the reigning Pope, and had fought to an issue for the Crown of the Holy Roman Empire, were conquered, humiliated and imprisoned by an upstart plebeian of Trastevere. The portcullis of Monte Giordano was lifted, and the mysterious gates were thrown wide to the curiosity of a populace drunk with victory; Giovanni degli Stefaneschi issued edicts of sovereign power from the sacred precincts of the Capitol; and the vagabond thieves of Rome feasted in the lordly halls of the Colonna palace. But though the tribune and the people could seize Rome, outnumbering the nobles as ten to one, they had neither the means nor the organization to besiege the fortified towns of the great houses, which hemmed in the city and the Campagna on every side. Thither the282 nobles retired to recruit fresh armies among their retainers, to forge new swords in their own smithies, and to concert new plans for recovering their ancient domination; and thence they returned in their strength, from their towers and their towns and fortresses, from Palestrina and Subiaco, Genazzano, San Vito and Paliano on the south, and from Bracciano and Galera and Anguillara, and all the Orsini castles on the north, to teach the people of Rome the great truth of those days, that 'aristocracy' meant not the careless supremacy of the nobly born, but the power of the strongest hands and the coolest heads to take and hold. Back came Colonna and Orsini, and the people, who a few months earlier had acclaimed their dictator in a fit of justifiable ill-temper against their masters, opened the gates for the nobles again, and no man lifted a hand to help Giovanni degli Stefaneschi, when the men-at-arms bound him and dragged him off to prison. Strange to say, no further vengeance was taken upon him, and for once in their history, the nobles shed no blood in revenge for a mortal injury.

No man could count the tragedies that swept over the Region of Ponte from the first outbreak of war between the Orsini and the Colonna, till Paolo Giordano Orsini, the last of the elder branch, breathed out his life in exile under the ban of Sixtus the Fifth, three hundred years later. There was no end of them till then, and there was little interruption of them while they lasted; there is no stone left standing from those days in that great quarter that may not have been splashed with their fierce blood, nor is there, perhaps, a church or chapel within their old holding into which an Orsini has not been borne dead or dying from some deadly fight. Even today it is gloomy, and the broad modern street, which swept down a straight harvest of memories through the quarter to the very Bridge of Sant' Angelo, has left the mediæval shadows on each side as dark as ever. Of the three parts of the city, which still recall the Middle Age most vividly, namely, the neighbourhood of San Pietro in Vincoli, in the first Region, the by-ways of Trastevere and the Region of Ponte, the latter is by far the most interesting. It was the abode of the Orsini; it was also the chief place of business for the bankers and money-changers who congregated there under the comparatively secure protection of the Guelph lords; and it was the quarter of prisons, of tortures, and of executions both secret and public. The names of the streets had terrible meaning: there was the Vicolo della Corda, and the Corda was the rope by which criminals were hoisted twenty feet in the air, and allowed to drop till their toes were just above the ground; there was the Piazza della Berlina Vecchia, the place of the Old Pillory; there was a little church known as the 'Church of the Gallows'; and there was a lane ominously called Vicolo dello Mastro; the Mastro was the Master of judicial executions, in other words, the Executioner284 himself. Before the Castle of Sant' Angelo stood the permanent gallows, rarely long unoccupied, and from an upper window of the dark Torre di Nona, on the hither side of the bridge, a rope hung swinging slowly in the wind, sometimes with a human body at the end of it, sometimes without. It was the place, and that was the manner, of executions that took place in the night. In Via di Monserrato stood the old fortress of the Savelli, long ago converted into a prison, and called the Corte Savella, the most terrible of all Roman dungeons for the horror of damp darkness, for ever associated with Beatrice Cenci's trial and death. Through those very streets she was taken in the cart to the little open space before the bridge, where she laid down her life upon the scaffold three hundred years ago, and left her story of offended innocence, of revenge and of expiation, which will not be forgotten while Rome is remembered.

Beatrice Cenci's story has been often told, but nowhere more clearly and justly than in Shelley's famous letter, written to explain his play. There are several manuscript accounts of the last scene at the Ponte Sant' Angelo, and I myself have lately read one, written by a contemporary and not elsewhere mentioned, but differing only from the rest in the horrible realism with which the picture is presented. The truth is plain enough; the unspeakable crimes of Francesco Cenci, his more than inhuman cruelty285 to his children and his wives, his monstrous lust and devilish nature, outdo anything to be found in any history of the world, not excepting the private lives of Tiberius, Nero, or Commodus. His daughter and his second wife killed him in his sleep. His death was merciful and swift, in an age when far less crimes were visited with tortures at the very name of which we shudder. They were driven to absolute desperation, and the world has forgiven them their one quick blow, struck for freedom, for woman's honour and for life itself in the dim castle of Petrella. Tormented with rack and cord they all confessed the deed, save Beatrice, whom no bodily pain could move; and if Paolo Santacroce had not murdered his mother for her money before their death was determined, Clement the Eighth would have pardoned them. But the times were evil, an example was called for, Santacroce had escaped to Brescia, and the Pope's heart was hardened against the Cenci.

BRIDGE OF SANT' ANGELO BRIDGE OF SANT' ANGELO

They died bravely, there at the head of the bridge, in the calm May morning, in the midst of a vast and restless crowd, among whom more than one person was killed by accident, as by the falling of a pot of flowers from a high window, and by the breaking down of a balcony over a shop, where too many had crowded in to see. The old house opposite looked down upon the scene, and the people watched Beatrice Cenci die from those same arched windows. Above the sea of faces, high on the wooden scaffold, rises the tall figure of a lovely girl, her hair gleaming in the sunshine like threads of dazzling gold, her marvellous blue eyes turned up to Heaven, her fresh young dimpled face not pale with fear, her exquisite lips moving softly as she repeats the De Profundis of her last appeal to God. Let the axe not fall. Let her stand there for ever in the spotless purity that cost her life on earth and set her name for ever among the high constellated stars of maidenly romance.

Close by the bridge, just opposite the Torre di Nona, stood the 'Lion Inn,' once kept by the beautiful287 Vanozza de Catanei, the mother of Rodrigo Borgia's children, of Cæsar, and Gandia, and Lucrezia, and the place was her property still when she was nominally married to her second husband, Carlo Canale, the keeper of the prison across the way. In the changing vicissitudes of the city, the Torre di Nona made way for the once famous Apollo Theatre, built upon the lower dungeons and foundations, and Faust's demon companion rose to the stage out of the depths that had heard the groans of tortured criminals; the theatre itself disappeared a few years ago in the works for improving the Tiber's banks, and a name is all that remains of a fact that made men tremble. In the late destruction, the old houses opposite were not altogether pulled down, but were sliced, as it were, through their roofs and rooms, at a safe angle; and there, no doubt, are still standing portions of Vanozza's inn, while far below, the cellars where she kept her wine free of excise, by papal privilege, are still as cool and silent as ever.

Not far beyond her hostelry stands another Inn, famous from early days and still open to such travellers as deign to accept its poor hospitality. It is an inn for the people now, for wine carters, and the better sort of hill peasants; it was once the best and most fashionable in Rome, and there the great Montaigne once dwelt, and is believed to have written at least a part of his famous Essay on Vanity. It is the Albergo dell'288 Orso, the 'Bear Inn,' and perhaps it is not a coincidence that Vanozza's sign of the Lion should have faced the approach to the Leonine City beyond the Tiber, and that the sign of the Bear, 'The Orsini Arms,' as an English innkeeper would christen it, should have been the principal resort of the kind in a quarter which was three-fourths the property and altogether the possession of the great house that overshadowed it, from Monte Giordano on the one side, and from Pompey's Theatre on the other.

The temporary fall of the Orsini at the end of the sixteenth century came about by one of the most extraordinary concatenations of events to be found in the chronicles. The story has filled more than one volume and is nevertheless very far from complete; nor is it possible, since the destruction of the Orsini archives, to reconstruct it with absolute accuracy. Briefly told, it is this.

Felice Peretti, monk and Cardinal of Montalto, and still nominally one of the so-called 'poor cardinals' who received from the Pope a daily allowance known as 'the Dish,' had nevertheless accumulated a good deal of property before he became Pope under the name of Sixtus the Fifth, and had brought some of his relatives to Rome. Among these was his well beloved nephew, Francesco Peretti, for whom he naturally sought an advantageous marriage. There was at that time in Rome a notary, named Accoramboni, a native289 of the Marches of Ancona and a man of some wealth and of good repute. He had one daughter, Vittoria, a girl of excessive vanity, as ambitious as she was vain and as singularly beautiful as she was ambitious. But she was also clever in a remarkable degree, and seems to have had no difficulty in hiding her bad qualities. Francesco Peretti fell in love with her, the Cardinal approved the match, though he was a man not easily deceived, and the two were married and settled in the Villa Negroni, which the Cardinal had built near the Baths of Diocletian. Having attained her first object, Vittoria took less pains to play the saint, and began to dress with unbecoming magnificence and to live on a very extravagant scale. Her name became a byword in Rome and her lovely face was one of the city's sights. The Cardinal, devotedly attached to his nephew, disapproved of the latter's young wife and regretted the many gifts he had bestowed upon her. Like most clever men, too, he was more than reasonably angry at having been deceived in his judgment of a girl's character. So far, there is nothing not commonplace about the tale.

At that time Paolo Giordano Orsini, the head of the house, Duke of Bracciano and lord of a hundred domains, was one of the greatest personages in Italy. No longer young and already enormously fat, he was married to Isabella de' Medici, the daughter of Cosimo, reigning in Florence. She was a beautiful and evil290 woman, and those who have endeavoured to make a martyr of her forget the nameless doings of her youth. Giordano was weak and extravagant, and paid little attention to his wife. She consoled herself with his kinsman, the young and handsome Troilo Orsini, who was as constantly at her side as an official 'cavalier servente' of later days. But the fat Giordano, indolent and pleasure seeking, saw nothing. Nor is there anything much more than vulgar and commonplace in all this.

Paolo Giordano meets Vittoria Peretti in Rome, and the two commonplaces begin the tragedy. On his part, love at first sight; ridiculous, at first, when one thinks of his vast bulk and advancing years, terrible, by and by, as the hereditary passions of his fierce race could be, backed by the almost boundless power which a great Italian lord possessed in his surroundings. Vittoria, tired of her dull and virtuous husband and of the lectures and parsimony of his uncle, and not dreaming that the latter was soon to be Pope, saw herself in a dream of glory controlling every mood and action of the greatest noble in the land. And she met Giordano again and again, and he pleaded and implored, and was alternately ridiculous and almost pathetic in his hopeless passion for the notary's daughter. But she had no thought of yielding to his entreaties. She would have marriage, or nothing. Neither words nor gifts could move her.

She had a husband, he had a wife; and she demanded that he should marry her, and was grimly silent as to the means. Until she was married to him he should not so much as touch the tips of her jewelled fingers, nor have a lock of her hair to wear in his bosom. He was blindly in love, and he was Paolo Giordano Orsini. It was not likely that he should hesitate. He who had seen nothing of his wife's doings, suddenly saw his kinsman, Troilo, and Isabella was doomed. Troilo fled to Paris, and Orsini took Isabella from Bracciano to the lonely castle of Galera. There he told her his mind and strangled her, as was his right, being feudal lord and master with powers of life and death. Then from Bracciano he sent messengers to kill Francesco Peretti. One of them had a slight acquaintance with the Cardinal's nephew.

They came to the Villa Negroni by night, and called him out, saying that his best friend was in need of him, and was waiting for him at Monte Cavallo. He hesitated, for it was very late. They had torches and weapons, and would protect him, they said. Still he wavered. Then Vittoria, his wife, scoffed at him, and called him coward, and thrust him out to die; for she knew. The men walked beside him with their torches, talking as they went. They passed the deserted land in the Baths of Diocletian, and turned at Saint Bernard's Church to go towards the Quirinal. Then they put out the lights and killed him quickly in the dark.

His body lay there all night, and when it was told the next day that Montalto's nephew had been murdered, the two men said that they had left him at Monte Cavallo and that he must have been killed as he came home alone. The Cardinal buried him without a word, and though he guessed the truth he asked neither vengeance nor justice of the Pope.

VILLA NEGRONI

From a print of the last century VILLA NEGRONI From a print of the last century

Gregory the Thirteenth guessed it, too, and when Orsini would have married Vittoria, the Pope forbade the banns and interdicted their union for ever. That much he dared to do against the greatest peer in the country.

To this, Orsini replied by plighting his faith to Vittoria with a ring, in the presence of a serving293 woman, an irregular ceremony which he afterwards described as a marriage, and he thereupon took his bride and her mother under his protection. The Pope retorted by a determined effort to arrest the murderers of Francesco; the Bargello and his men went in the evening to the Orsini palace at Pompey's Theatre and demanded that Giordano should give up the criminals; the porter replied that the Duke was asleep; the Orsini men-at-arms lunged out with their weapons, looked on during the interview, and considering the presence of the Bargello derogatory to their master, drove him away, killing one of his men and wounding several others. Thereupon Pope Gregory forbade the Duke from seeing Vittoria or communicating with her by messengers, on pain of a fine of ten thousand gold ducats, an order to which Orsini would have paid no attention but which Vittoria was too prudent to disregard, and she retired to her brother's house, leaving the Duke in a state of frenzied rage that threatened insanity. Then the Pope seemed to waver again, and then again learning that the lovers saw each other constantly in spite of his commands, he suddenly had Vittoria seized and imprisoned in Sant' Angelo. It is impossible to follow the long struggle that ensued. It lasted four years, at the end of which time the Duke and Vittoria were living at Bracciano, where the Orsini was absolute lord and master and beyond the jurisdiction of the Church —two hours' ride294 from the gates of Rome. But no further formality of marriage had taken place and Vittoria was not satisfied. Then Gregory the Thirteenth died.

During the vacancy of the Holy See, all interdictions of the late Pope were suspended. Instantly Giordano determined to be married, and came to Rome with Vittoria. They believed that the Conclave would last some time and were making their arrangements without haste, living in Pompey's Theatre, when a messenger brought word that Cardinal Montalto would surely be elected Pope within a few hours. In the fortress is the small family church of Santa Maria di Grotta Pinta. The Duke sent down word to his chaplain that the latter must marry him at once. That night a retainer of the house had been found murdered at the gate; his body lay on a trestle bier before the altar of the chapel when the Duke's message came; the Duke himself and Vittoria were already in the little winding stair that leads down from the apartments; there was not a moment to be lost; the frightened chaplain and the messenger hurriedly raised a marble slab which closed an unused vault, dropped the murdered man's body into the chasm, and had scarcely replaced the stone when the ducal pair entered the church. The priest married them before the altar in fear and trembling, and when they were gone entered the whole story in the little register in the sacristy. The leaf is extant.

Within a few hours, Montalto was Pope, the humble cardinal was changed in a moment to the despotic pontiff, whose nephew's murder was unavenged; instead of the vacillating Gregory, Orsini had to face the terrible Sixtus, and his defeat and exile were foregone conclusions. He could no longer hold his own and he took refuge in the States of Venice, where his kinsman, Ludovico, was a fortunate general. He made a will which divided his personal estate between Vittoria and his son, Virginio, greatly to the woman's advantage; and overcome by the infirmity of his monstrous size, spent by the terrible passions of his later years, and broken in heart by an edict of exile which he could no longer defy, he died at Salò within seven months of his great enemy's coronation, in the forty-ninth year of his age.

Vittoria retired to Padua, and the authorities declared the inheritance valid, but Ludovico Orsini's long standing hatred of her was inflamed to madness by the conditions of the will. Six weeks after the Duke's death, at evening, Vittoria was in her chamber; her boy brother, Flaminio, was singing a Miserere to his lute by the fire in the great hall. A sound of quick feet, the glare of torches, and Ludovico's masked men filled the house. Vittoria died bravely with one deep stab in her heart. The boy, Flaminio, was torn to pieces with seventy-four wounds.

But Venice would permit no such outrageous deeds. Ludovico was besieged in his house, by horse and foot and artillery, and was taken alive with many of his men and swiftly conveyed to Venice; and a week had not passed from the day of the murder before he was strangled by the Bargello in the latter's own room, with the red silk cord by which it was a noble's privilege to die. The first one broke, and they had to take another, but Ludovico Orsini did not wince. An hour later his body was borne out with forty torches, in solemn procession, to lie in state in Saint Mark's Church. His men were done to death with hideous tortures in the public square. So ended the story of Vittoria Accoramboni.

REGION VI PARIONE

The principal point of this Region is Piazza Navona, which exactly coincides with Domitian's race-course, and the Region consists of an irregular triangle of which the huge square is at the northern angle, the western one being the Piazza della Chiesa Nuova and the southern extremity the theatre of Pompey, so often referred to in these pages as one of the Orsini's strongholds and containing the little church in which Paolo Giordano married Vittoria

Accoramboni, close to the Campo dei Fiori which was the place of public executions by fire. The name Parione is said to be derived from the Latin 'Paries,' a wall, applied to a massive remnant of ancient masonry which once stood298 somewhere in the Via di Parione. It matters little; nor can we find any satisfactory explanation of the gryphon which serves as a device for the whole quarter, included during the Middle Age, with Ponte and Regola, in the large portion of the city dominated by the Orsini.

The Befana, which is a corruption of Epifania, the Feast of the Epiphany, is and always has been the season of giving presents in Rome, corresponding with our Christmas; and the Befana is personated as a gruff old woman who brings gifts to little children after the manner of our Saint Nicholas. But in the minds of Romans, from earliest childhood, the name is associated with the night fair, opened on the eve of the Epiphany in Piazza Navona, and which was certainly one of the most extraordinary popular festivals ever invented to amuse children and make children of grown people, a sort of foreshadowing of Carnival, but having at the same time a flavour and a colour of its own, unlike anything else in the world.

During the days after Christmas a regular line of booths is erected, encircling the whole circus-shaped space. It is a peculiarity of Roman festivals that all the material for adornment is kept together from year to year, ready for use at a moment's notice, and when one sees the enormous amount of lumber required for the Carnival, for the fireworks on the Pincio, or for the Befana, one cannot help wondering where it is all kept. From year to year it lies somewhere, in those vast subterranean places and great empty houses used for that especial purpose, of which only Romans guess the extent. When needed, it is suddenly produced without confusion, marked and numbered, ready to be put together and regilt or repainted, or hung with the acres of draperies which Latins know so well how to display in everything approaching to public pageantry.

At dark, on the Eve of the Epiphany, the Befana begins. The hundreds of booths are choked with toys and gleam with thousands of little lights, the open spaces are thronged by a moving crowd, the air splits with the infernal din of ten thousand whistles and tin trumpets. Noise is the first consideration for a successful befana, noise of any kind, shrill, gruff, high, low—any sort of noise; and the first purchase of everyone who comes must be a tin horn, a pipe, or one of those grotesque little figures of painted earthenware, representing some characteristic type of Roman life and having a whistle attached to it, so cleverly modelled in the clay as to produce the most hideous noises without even the addition of a wooden plug. But anything will do. On a memorable night nearly thirty years ago, the whole cornopean stop of an organ was sold in the fair, amounting to seventy or eighty pipes with their reeds. The instrument in the old English Protestant Church outside of Porta del Popolo had been improved, and the organist, who was a practical Anglo-Saxon, conceived300 the original and economical idea of selling the useless pipes at the night fair for the benefit of the church. The braying of the high, cracked reeds was frightful and never to be forgotten.

Round and round the square, three generations of families, children, parents and even grandparents, move in a regular stream, closer and closer towards midnight and supper-time; nor is the place deserted till three o'clock in the morning. Toys everywhere, original with an attractive ugliness, nine-tenths of them made of earthenware dashed with a kind of bright and harmless paint of which every Roman child remembers the taste for life; and old and young and middle-aged all blow their whistles and horns with solemnly ridiculous pertinacity, pausing only to make some little purchase at the booths, or to exchange a greeting with passing friends, followed by an especially vigorous burst of noise as the whistles are brought close to each other's ears, and the party that can make the more atrocious din drives the other half deafened from the field. And the old women who help to keep the booths sit warming their skinny hands over earthen pots of coals and looking on without a smile on their Sibylline faces, while their sons and daughters sell clay hunchbacks and little old women of clay, the counterparts of their mothers, to the passing customers. Thousands upon thousands of people throng the place, and it is warm with the presence of so much humanity, even under the301 clear winter sky. And there is no confusion, no accident, no trouble, there are no drunken men and no pickpockets. But Romans are not like other people.

In a few days all is cleared away again, and Bernini's great fountain faces Borromini's big Church of Saint Agnes, in the silence; and the officious guide tells the credulous foreigner how the figure of the Nile in the group is veiling his head to hide the sight of the hideous architecture, and how the face of the Danube expresses the River God's terror lest the tower should fall upon him; and how the architect retorted upon the sculptor by placing Saint Agnes on the summit of the church, in the act of reassuring the Romans as to the safety of her shrine; and again, how Bernini's enemies said that the obelisk of the fountain was tottering, till he came alone on foot and tied four lengths of twine to the four corners of the pedestal, and fastened the strings to the nearest houses, in derision, and went away laughing. It was at that time that he modelled four grinning masks for the corners of his sedan-chair, so that they seemed to be making scornful grimaces at his detractors as he was carried along. He could afford to laugh. He had been the favourite of Urban the Eighth who, when Cardinal Barberini, had actually held the looking-glass by the aid of which the handsome young sculptor modelled his own portrait in the figure of David with the sling, now in the Museum of Villa Borghese. After a brief period of disgrace under the next reign, brought about by the sharpness of his Neapolitan tongue, Bernini was restored to the favour of Innocent the Tenth, the Pamfili Pope, to please whose economical tastes he executed the fountain in Piazza Navona, after a design greatly reduced in extent as well as in beauty, compared with the first he had sketched. But an account of Bernini would lead far and profit little; the catalogue of his works would fill a small volume; and after all, he was successful only in an age when art had fallen low. In place of Michelangelo's universal genius, Bernini possessed a born Neapolitan's universal facility. He could do something of everything, circumstances gave him enormous opportunities, and there were few things which he did not attempt, from classic sculpture to the final architecture of Saint Peter's and the fortifications of Sant' Angelo. He was afflicted by the hereditary giantism of the Latins, and was often moved by motives of petty spite against his inferior rival, Borromini. His best work is the statue of Saint Teresa in Santa Maria della Vittoria, a figure which has recently excited the ecstatic admiration of a French critic, expressed in language that betrays at once the fault of the conception, the taste of the age in which Bernini lived, and the unhealthy nature of the sculptor's prolific talent. Only the seventeenth century could have represented such a disquieting fusion of the sensuous and the spiritual, and it was reserved for the decadence of our own days to find words that could describe it. Bernini has been praised as the Michelangelo of his day, but no one has yet been bold enough, or foolish enough, to call Michelangelo the Bernini of the sixteenth century. Barely sixty years elapsed between the death of the one and birth of the other, and the space of a single lifetime separates the zenith of the Renascence from the nadir of Barocco art.

PIAZZA NAVONA PIAZZA NAVONA

The names of Bernini and of Piazza Navona recall Innocent the Tenth, who built the palace beside the Church of Saint Agnes, his meannesses, his nepotism, his weakness, and his miserable end; how his relatives stripped him of all they could lay hands on, and how at the last, when he died in the only shirt he possessed, covered by a single ragged blanket, his sister-in-law, Olimpia Maldachini, dragged from beneath his pallet bed the two small chests of money which he had succeeded in concealing to the end. A brass candlestick with a single burning taper stood beside him in his last moments, and before he was quite dead, a servant stole it and put a wooden one in its place. When he was dead at the Quirinal, his body was carried to Saint Peter's in a bier so short that the poor Pope's feet stuck out over the end, and three days later, no one could be found to pay for the burial. Olimpia declared that she was a starving widow and could do nothing; the corpse was thrust into a place where the masons of the Vatican kept their tools, and one of the workmen, out of charity or superstition, lit a tallow candle beside it. In the end, the maggiordomo paid for a deal coffin, and Monsignor Segni gave five scudi—an English pound—to have the body taken away and buried. It was slung between two mules and taken by night to the Church of Saint Agnes, where in the changing course of human and domestic events, it ultimately got an expensive monument in the worst possible taste. The learned and sometimes witty Baracconi, who has set down the story, notes the fact that Leo the Tenth, Pius the Fourth and Gregory the Sixteenth fared little better in their obsequies, and he comments upon the democratic spirit of a city in which such things can happen.

Close to the Piazza Navona stands the famous mutilated group, known as Pasquino, of which the mere name conveys a better idea of the Roman character than volumes of description, for it was here that the pasquinades were published, by affixing them to a pedestal at the corner of the Palazzo Braschi. And one of Pasquino's bitterest jests was directed against Olimpia Maldachini. Her name was cut in two, to make a good Latin pun: 'Olim pia, nunc impia,' 'once pious, now impious,' or 'Olimpia, now impious,' as one chose to join or separate the syllables. Whole books have been filled with the short and pithy imaginary conversations between Marforio, the statue of a river god which used to stand in the Monti, and Pasquino, beneath whom the Roman children used to be told that the book of all wisdom was buried for ever.

In the Region of Parione stands the famous Cancelleria, a masterpiece of Bramante's architecture, celebrated for many events in the later history of Rome, and successively the princely residence of several cardinals, chief of whom was that strong Pompeo Colonna, the ally of the Emperor Charles the Fifth, who was responsible for the sacking of Rome by the Constable of Bourbon, who ultimately ruined the Holy League, and imposed his terrible terms of peace upon Clement the Seventh, a prisoner in Sant' Angelo. Considering the devastation and the horrors which were the result of that contest, and its importance in Rome's history, it is worth while to tell the story again. Connected with it was the last great struggle between Orsini and Colonna, Orsini, as usual, siding for the Pope, and therefore for the Holy League, and Colonna for the Emperor.

Charles the Fifth had vanquished Francis the First at Pavia, in the year , and had taken the French King prisoner. A year later the Holy League was formed, between Pope Clement the Seventh, the King of France, the Republics of Venice and Florence, and Francesco Sforza, Duke of Milan. Its object was to fight the Emperor, to sustain Sforza, and to seize the Kingdom of Naples by force. Immediately upon the proclamation of the League, the Emperor's ambassadors left Rome, the Colonna retired to their strongholds, and the Emperor made preparations to send Charles, Duke of Bourbon, the disgraced relative of King Francis, to storm Rome and reduce the imprisoned Pope to submission. The latter's first and nearest source of fear lay in the Colonna, who held the fortresses and passes between Rome and the Neapolitan frontier, and his first instinct was to attack them with the help of the Orsini. But neither side was ready for the fight, and the timid Pontiff eagerly accepted the promise of peace made by the Colonna in order to gain time, and he dismissed the forces he had hastily raised against them.

PALAZZO MASSIMO ALLE COLONNA PALAZZO MASSIMO ALLE COLONNA
PONTE SISTO

From a print of the last century PONTE SISTO From a print of the last century They, in the mean time, treated with Moncada, Regent of Naples for the Emperor, and at once seized Anagni, put several thousand men in the field, marched upon Rome with incredible speed, seized three gates in the night, and entered the city in triumph on the following morning. The Pope and the Orsini, completely taken by surprise, offered little or no resistance. According to some writers, it was Pompeo Colonna's daring plan to murder the Pope, force his own election to the Pontificate by arms, destroy the Orsini, and open Rome to Charles the Fifth; and when the Colonna advanced on the same day, by Ponte Sisto, to Trastevere, and threatened to attack Saint Peter's and the Vatican, Clement the Seventh, remembering Sciarra and Pope Boniface, was308 on the point of imitating the latter and arraying himself in his Pontifical robes to await his enemy with such dignity as he could command. But the remonstrances of the more prudent cardinals prevailed, and about noon they conveyed him safely to Sant' Angelo by the secret covered passage, leaving the Colonna to sack Trastevere and even Saint Peter's itself, though they dared not come too near to Sant' Angelo for fear of its cannons. The tumult over at last, Don Ugo de Moncada, in the Emperor's name, took possession of the Pope's two nephews as hostages for his own safety, entered Sant' Angelo under a truce, and stated the Emperor's conditions of peace. These were, to all intents and purposes, that the Pope should withdraw his troops, wherever he had any, and that the Emperor should be free to advance wherever he pleased, except through the Papal States, that the Pope should give hostages for his good faith, and that he should grant a free pardon to all the Colonna, who vaguely agreed to withdraw their forces into the Kingdom of Naples. To this humiliating peace, or armistice, for it was nothing more, the Pope was forced by the prospect of starvation, and he would even have agreed to sail to Barcelona in order to confer with the Emperor; but from this he was ultimately dissuaded by Henry the Eighth of England and the King of France, 'who sent him certain sums of money and promised him their support.' The consequence was that he broke the truce as soon as he309 dared, deprived the Cardinal of his hat, and, with the help of the Orsini, attacked the Colonna by surprise on their estates, giving orders to burn their castles and raze their fortresses to the ground. Four villages were burned before the surprised party could recover itself; but with some assistance from the imperial troops they were soon able to face their enemies on equal terms, and the little war raged fiercely during several months, with varying success and all possible cruelty on both sides.

Meanwhile Charles, Duke of Bourbon, known as the Constable, and more or less in the pay of the Emperor, had gathered an army in Lombardy. His force consisted of the most atrocious ruffians of the time,—Lutheran Germans, superstitious Spaniards, revolutionary Italians, and such other nondescripts as would join his standard,—all fellows who had in reality neither country nor conscience, and were ready to serve any soldier of fortune who promised them plunder and license. The predominating element was Spanish, but there was not much to choose among them all so far as their instincts were concerned. Charles was penniless, as usual; he offered his horde of cutthroats the rich spoils of Tuscany and Rome, they swore to follow him to death and perdition, and he began his southward march. The Emperor looked on with an approving eye, and the Pope was overcome by abject terror. In the vain hope of saving himself310 and the city he concluded a truce with the Viceroy of Naples, agreeing to pay sixty thousand ducats, to give back everything taken from the Colonna, and to restore Pompeo to the honours of the cardinalate. The conditions of the armistice were forthwith carried out, by the disbanding of the Pope's hired soldiers and the payment of the indemnity, and Clement the Seventh enjoyed during a few weeks the pleasant illusion of fancied safety.

He awoke from the dream, in horror and fear, to find that the Constable considered himself in no way bound by a peace concluded with the Emperor's Viceroy, and was advancing rapidly upon Rome, ravaging and burning everything in his way. Hasty preparations for defence were made; a certain Renzo da Ceri armed such men as he could enlist with such weapons as he could find, and sent out a little force of grooms and artificers to face the Constable's ruthless Spaniards and the fierce Germans of his companion freebooter, George of Fransperg, or Franzberg, who carried about a silken cord by which he swore to strangle the Pope with his own hands. The enemy reached the walls of Rome on the night of the fifth of May; devastation and famine lay behind them in their track, the plunder of the Church was behind the walls, and far from northward came rumours of the army of the League on its way to cut off their retreat. They resolved to win the spoil or die, and at dawn the Constable, clad in a white cloak, led the assault and set up the first scaling ladder, close to the Porta San Spirito. In the very act a bullet struck him in a vital part and he fell headlong to the earth. Benvenuto Cellini claimed the credit of the shot, but it is more than probable that it sped from another hand, that of Bernardino Passeri; it matters little now, it mattered less then, as the infuriated Spaniards stormed the walls in the face of Camillo Orsini's desperate and hopeless resistance, yelling 'Blood and the Bourbon,' for a war-cry.

Once more the wretched Pope fled along the secret corridor with his cardinals, his prelates and his servants; for although he might yet have escaped from the doomed city, messengers had brought word that Cardinal Pompeo Colonna had ten thousand men-at-arms in the Campagna, ready to cut off his flight, and he was condemned to be a terrified spectator of Rome's destruction from the summit of a fortress which he dared not surrender and could hardly hope to defend. Seven thousand Romans were slaughtered in the storming of the walls; the enemy gained all Trastevere at a blow and the sack began; the torrent of fury poured across Ponte Sisto into Rome itself, thousands upon thousands of steel-clad madmen, drunk with blood and mad with the glitter of gold, a storm of unimaginable terror. Cardinals, Princes and Ambassadors were dragged from their palaces, and when greedy hands had gathered up all that could be taken away, fire consumed the rest, and the miserable captives were tortured into promising fabulous ransoms for life and limb. Abbots, priors and heads of religious orders were treated with like barbarity, and the few who escaped the clutches of the bloodthirsty Spanish soldiers fell into the reeking hands of the brutal German adventurers. The enormous sum of six million ducats was gathered together in value of gold and silver bullion and of precious things, and as much more was extorted as promised ransom from the gentlemen and churchmen and merchants of Rome by the savage tortures of the lash, the iron boot and the rack. The churches were stripped of all consecrated vessels, the Sacred Wafers were scattered abroad by the Catholic Spaniards and trampled in the bloody ooze that filled the ways, the convents were stormed by a rabble in arms and the nuns were distributed as booty among their fiendish captors, mothers and children were slaughtered in the streets and drunken Spaniards played dice for the daughters of honourable citizens.

From the surrounding Campagna the Colonna entered the city in arms, orderly, silent and sober, and from their well-guarded fortresses they contemplated the ruin they had brought upon Rome. Cardinal Pompeo installed himself in his palace of the Cancelleria in the Region of Parione, and gave shelter to such of his friends as might be useful to him thereafter. In revenge upon John de'

Medici, the Captain of the Black Bands, whose assistance the Pope had invoked, the Cardinal caused the Villa Medici on Monte Mario to be burned to the ground, and Clement the Seventh watched the flames from the ramparts of Sant' Angelo. One good action is recorded of the savage churchman. He ransomed and protected in his house the wife and the daughter of that Giorgio Santacroce who had murdered the Cardinal's father by night, when the Cardinal himself was an infant in arms, more than forty years earlier; and he helped some of his friends to escape by a chimney from the room in which they had been confined and tortured into promising a ransom they could not pay. But beyond those few acts he did little to mitigate the horrors of the month-long sack, and nothing to relieve the city from the yoke of its terrible captors. The Holy League sent a small force to the Pope's assistance and it reached the gates of Rome; but the Spaniards were in possession of immense stores of ammunition and provisions, they had more horses than they needed and more arms than they could bear; the forces of the League had traversed a country in which not a blade of grass had been left undevoured nor a measure of corn uneaten; and the avengers of the dead Constable, securely fortified within the walls, looked down with contempt upon an army already decimated by sickness and starvation.

At this juncture, Clement the Seventh resolved to abandon further resistance and sue for peace. The guns of Sant' Angelo had all but fired their last shot, and the supply of food was nearly exhausted, when the Pope sent for Cardinal Colonna; the churchman consented to a parley, and the man who had suffered confiscation and disgrace entered the castle as the arbiter of destiny. He was received as the mediator of peace and a benefactor of humanity, and when he stated his terms they were not refused. The Pope and the thirteen Cardinals who were with him were to remain prisoners until the payment of four hundred thousand ducats of gold, after which they were to be conducted to Naples to await the further pleasure of the Emperor; the Colonna were to be absolutely and freely pardoned for all they had done; in the hope of some subsequent assistance the Pope promised to make Cardinal Colonna the Legate of the Marches. As a hostage for the performance of these and other conditions, Cardinal Orsini was delivered over to his enemy, who conducted him as his prisoner to the Castle of Grottaferrata, and the Colonna secretly agreed to allow the Pope to go free from Sant' Angelo. On the night of December the ninth, seven months after the storming of the city, the head of the Holy Roman Catholic and Apostolic Church fled from the castle in the humble garb of a market gardener, and made good his escape to Orvieto and to the protection of the Holy League.

Meanwhile a pestilence had broken out in Rome, and the spectre of a mysterious and mortal sickness distracted those who had survived the terrors of sword and flame. The Spanish and German soldiery either fell victims to the plague or deserted in haste and fear; and though Cardinal Pompeo's peace contained no promise that the city should be evacuated, it was afterwards stated upon credible authority that, within two years from their coming, not one of the barbarous horde was left alive within the walls. When all was over the city was little more than a heap of ruins, but the Colonna had been victorious, and were sated with revenge. This, in brief, is the history of the storming and sacking of Rome which took place in the year , at the highest development of the Renascence, in the youth of Benvenuto Cellini, when Michelangelo had not yet painted the Last Judgment, when Titian was just fifty years old, and when Raphael and Lionardo da Vinci were but lately dead; and the contrast between the sublimity of art and the barbarity of human nature in that day is only paralleled in the annals of our own century, at once the bloodiest and the most civilized in the history of the world.

The Cancelleria, wherein Pompeo Colonna sheltered the wife and daughter of his father's murderer, is remembered for some modern political events: for the opening of the first representative parliament under Pius the Ninth, in , for the assassination of the Pope's minister, Pellegrino Rossi, on the steps of the entrance in the same year, and as the place where the so-called Roman Republic was proclaimed in . But it is most of all interesting for the nobility of its proportions and the simplicity of its architecture. It is undeniably, and almost undeniedly, the best building in Rome today, though that may not be saying much in a city which has been more exclusively the prey of the Barocco than any other.

THE CANCELLERIA THE CANCELLERIA

The Palace of the Massimo, once built to follow the curve of a narrow winding street, but now facing the same great thoroughfare as the Cancelleria, has something of the same quality, with a wholly different character.

It is smaller and more gloomy, and its columns317 are almost black with age; it was here, in , that Pannartz and Schweinheim, two of those nomadic German scholars who have not yet forgotten the road to Italy, established their printing-press in the house of Pietro de' Massimi, and here took place one of those many romantic tragedies which darkened the end of the sixteenth century. For a certain Signore Massimo, in the year , had been married and had eight sons, mostly grown men, when he fell in love with a light-hearted lady of more wit than virtue, and announced that he would make her his wife, though his sons warned him that they would not bear the slight upon their mother's memory.

The old man, infatuated and beside himself with love, would not listen to them, but published the banns, married the woman, and brought her home for his wife.

One of the sons, the youngest, was too timid to join the rest; but on the next morning the seven others went to the bridal apartment, and killed their stepmother when their father was away.

But he came back before she was quite dead, and he took the Crucifix from the wall by the bed and cursed his children. And the curse was fulfilled upon them.

Parione is the heart of Mediæval Rome, the very centre of that black cloud of mystery which hangs over the city of the Middle Age. A history might be composed out of Pasquin's sayings, volumes have been written about Cardinal Pompeo Colonna and the ruin he318 wrought, whole books have been filled with the life and teachings and miracles of Saint Philip Neri, who belonged to this quarter, erected here his great oratory, and is believed to have recalled from the dead a youth of the house of Massimo in that same gloomy palace.

The story of Rome is a tale of murder and sudden death, varied, changing, never repeated in the same way; there is blood on every threshold; a tragedy lies buried in every church and chapel; and again we ask in vain wherein lies the magic of the city that has fed on terror and grown old in carnage, the charm that draws men to her,

the power that holds, the magic that enthralls men soul and body, as Lady Venus cast her spells upon Tannhäuser in her mountain of old.

Yet none deny it, and as centuries roll on, the poets, the men of letters, the musicians, the artists of all ages, have come to her from far countries and have dwelt here while they might, some for long years, some for the few months they could spare; and all of them have left something, a verse, a line, a sketch, a song that breathes the threefold mystery of love, eternity and death.
